The Power of Inclusion:

Meditating with Compassion,
Healing with Generosity,
Leading with Love

Cecilia B. Loving

Myrtle Tree Press

BROOKLYN, NEW YORK

Copyright © 2021 by Cecilia B. Loving
All rights reserved
Printed in the United States of America

Myrtle Tree Press LLC
Brooklyn, New York
https://www.amazon.com – Author's Page: Cecilia B. Loving

Publisher's Note: No part of this publication,
including its artwork,
may be reproduced, stored in a retrieval system,
or transmitted, in any form or by any means,
electronic, imaging, mechanical,
photocopying, digital, recording, scanning,
or otherwise, without the written
prior permission of the author.

The Power of Inclusion: Meditating with Compassion,
Healing with Generosity, Leading with Love /
Cecilia B. Loving — First Edition

ISBN 978-0-9860088-8-7 (paperback) |
ISBN 978-0-9860088-4-9 (ebook) |
Library of Congress Control Number: 2021909449

Praise for *THE POWER OF INCLUSION*

"*The Power of Inclusion* brings the whispers of the ancestors to my heart and soul. The words move like a river, reminding me that we are all in a flow with each other and more connected in every moment than we can imagine. It is an invitation to transform our way of experiencing the world.

We are invited to see the beauty within us and recognize the beauty of the other. In doing so, we see that we change and are changed in every encounter, no matter how seemingly insignificant that encounter may be.

The call to meditation brought me to the waters of the world, its streams, rivers, and oceans. It brought me to the mirroring in me of the waters flowing through my veins and arteries in a dance of intricate connection. What happens to the water happens to me in a circle.

This is a book we will treasure for a lifetime, to be savored, to prompt reflection, to inspire connection and bonding with all that is, seen and unseen."

Grandmother Strong Oak,
Visioning B.E.A.R. Circle, Intertribal Coalition, Inc.

"Cecilia's heart and spirit shine brightly through these pages. Her words and stories move my soul, so I was compelled to read these pages in one sitting. She provides powerful gifts in both the inspirational lessons and mindful practices dispersed throughout this beautiful book. I am grateful to know her."

Lisa Podemski, Esq., Yoga, Reiki and Mindfulness Expert,
NYC Bar Mindfulness & Well-Being Committee Chair (2021-24)

"Cecilia Loving has a gift for opening up windows and doors on the Mystery that is both inside us and beyond us. *The Power of Inclusion* is among her best works yet. Be prepared to experience a compelling invitation to walk through the doorway of love into a new world of candor and compassion."

Rev. Dr. Dale T. Irvin
Professor, World Christianity, New School of Biblical Theology

"Cecilia has gifted us with a contemplative guide with *The Power of Inclusion* to help discover where we are on the journey of inclusion. Whether you work in diversity, equity, accessibility and inclusion or are just curious about your own discomfort, this book is a companion for you."

Monika L. Son, Ph.D., Contemplative Scholar, Educator, Writer,
and Embodied Leadership Coach

THE POWER OF INCLUSION

"Cecilia Loving beautifully describes the profound truth that
our lives are all interconnected, and the inclusive love
that is the heart's response to that truth.
The book is uplifting, inspiring, and practical,
all at the same time."

Sharon Salzberg,
Author of *Lovingkindness* and *Real Change*

"This book is timely in the world we live in today.
Cecilia brilliantly shares strategies on how we can all be more
inclusive to everyone around us. The book is excellent, and I
highly recommend everyone, especially those interested in the
Diversity, Equity and Inclusion field, to read it."

Laurie Robinson Haden
CEO, Corporate Counsel Women of Color

"*The Power of Inclusion* reminds us that the muscle of love can
expand within us to include, embrace, empower and uplift all
those within our purview and that we are all stronger and
better when it does. We need this book today to help us chart
our paths forward toward more good and light in the world."

Rhonda Joy McLean
Author, *The Little Black Book of Success*

"As instructive as it is powerful and inspiring, in *The Power of Inclusion*, Loving guides the reader through a step-by-step spiritual journey to building a kinder and more compassionate world—starting from within."

Jordana Alter Confino, Adjunct Professor of Law,
and Expert in Positive Psychology and Lawyer Well-Being

"Rev. Dr. Cecilia Loving has once more demonstrated her amazing gifts of insight, spirituality, and writing. By the power of her words, she reinforces the message that we are one. In Spirit, there is no race, ethnicity, creed, or gender identities. We are one in Spirit. Thank you, Reverend Loving, for your truth, wisdom, and understanding."

The Honorable Charlotte D. Brown, Immigration Judge

"Cecilia reminds us to be mindful of the unfailing strength with which humanity will thrive so long as inclusion is established and maintained as the pillar of this our global community."

Atoia Scott, Healer, Circle Keeper, Prayer Warrior

THE POWER OF INCLUSION

"Cecilia Loving's book *The Power of Inclusion* is part manifesto, part self-help guide, and part instruction manual for fostering inclusion in the workplace—and in the world. Cecilia shows us how universal principles of love, oneness, and mindfulness can help us realize that we're all connected. In that moment, inclusion becomes the only natural human response. Drawing liberally from the wisdom of her elders, from Native American lore, from diverse writers from around the world and across time, and from the latest science, she weaves a compelling narrative that guides us in how to bring out the best in ourselves and each other."

Dr. Larry Richard, LawyerBrain LLC
Improving Lawyer Performance Through Personality Science

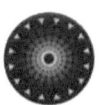

"In *The Power of Inclusion*, Cecilia B. Loving helps us to see what has been missing from costly and well-intentioned diversity and inclusion initiatives, many of which fail miserably or are unsustainable. They fail to encompass matters of the heart or spirit/love, which we do not like to discuss in the workplace. Loving helps us to see that to have successful and sustainable 'diversity, equity, accessibility, and inclusive (DEAI)' programs, we must see that we are all connected. We are one."

Sabrina A. Griffin, Diversity, Equity & Inclusion Expert,
Former Diversity Manager, Chubb Group of Insurance Companies

"Cecilia's words are a healing balm for the soul. These words will inspire you, offer you guidance, and bring you relief to imagine what is possible for you and for our world."

Anu Gupta, Founder & CEO, BE MORE with Anu

"Thank you, Cecilia, for this thoughtful, insightful, and amazing resource. Since knowing you for over 25 years, you have been a steadfast champion of inclusion— always bringing a holistic and inclusive lens as you walk the talk."

Anna L. Brown, Chief Inclusion & Diversity Officer
Baker & McKenzie LLP

"Cecilia's words are like a healing balm, tenderly calling our souls into a life-giving oasis. It takes skill to speak truth in the perfect balance of love and courage. *The Power of Inclusion* is a gift and an invitation to journey along a transformative path. Readers will return to it again and again
for its ancient/new wisdom."

Jason Craige Harris, Perception Institute

THE POWER OF INCLUSION

Dedicated to
everyone who continues to support
the power of inclusion,
especially
Myrtle, Marlon, Pat, Mary, Gina, Wendy, Tameka,
Michael, Giselle, Kobie, Brooke, Sabrina, Anna, Nandar,
Joy, Prentis, David, Larry, Steven, Vaughn, Andrew,
Kenny, Kobie, Tray, Jon, Greg, Telina, Dellon, Charlotte,
Alonzo, Ali, Yomi, Lea, Will, Ben, Jason, Sharon,
Atoia, Darius, Lester, Malcolm, Kia, Valerie, Monika,
Grandmother Strong Oak, Bob, Suzanne, Hilary,
Michelle, Dena, Bella, JAC, Quynh, Raquiba,
Carmelyn, Nicole, Chanda, Ramla, Nelson, Sam,
Vanessa, Johanna, Kimera, Laurie, Lisa, Larry,
the DEI Public Service Thought Leaders,
the Corporate Counsel Women of Color,
Jordana, Jamie, Julia, Laura, Rhonda Joy, Elizabeth,
Dan, John, Tom, Mark, Lillian, Grace, Alvin,
and everyone else
who stays the course
of this journey
without end.

Contents

I. MEDITATING WITH COMPASSION 1

Welcome 3

Honor 19

Meditate 39

Listen 53

II. HEALING WITH GENEROSITY 57

Circle 59

Share 67

Forgive 73

Thank 77

Balance 81

III. LEADING WITH LOVE 119

Lead 121

Begin 155

Love 173

RESOURCES 195

ABOUT THE AUTHOR 199

*Beyond a table to share
or invitation to dance,
is a muscle of love,
that grows stronger
welcoming differences
as the absolute good
that cherishes all of us.*

I.

MEDITATING WITH COMPASSION

The power of inclusion
stretches beyond fear
to center in the breath
we all breathe,
with the centrifugal force
of love.

CHAPTER 1

Welcome

Inclusion welcomes all
with a heart that gives
without asking to receive,
exercising its muscle of compassion
to invite everyone in,
trusting the oneness that we share,
everywhere, every place, every time.

Regardless of what brought you to these pages, you are in your right place, at your right time. We all bring something amazing to this journey that we call life. Inclusion is one of our most powerful gifts. As we open the door to a new season and try to make a difference in a world struggling to improve itself, the most important thing we bring is the truth that we are one. Oneness is the greatest lesson of the pandemic and the only way to dispel the ugliness of racism and hatred. Separation is an illusion.

When one being suffers, we all do. Yet, as much as we are vulnerable to physical dis-ease, we are also healed by the compassion, kindness, and peace we share.

This book is not a typical journey exploring diversity, equity, accessibility, and inclusion as though they were a quick fix rather than an involved spiritual process. In many respects, this book is a prayer for our journey through this wilderness. We will pause along the way to remind you of our connection: I am blessed by you, and you are blessed by me.

We are mirrors of each other's infinite potential. Because of the positive energy you express through your unique presence and perspective, the world is a better place. Even what is intended for negativity will be transformed into good because the universe conspires to help us. The soul thrives in knowing we are here for each other. There is nothing that I expect from you except the full expression of who you are, which makes the world better.

If our lives are the proverbial table to which we invite others, then our generosity, love, and forgiveness are the sustenance we share with each other. We know in our hearts that our gifts are not just for us individually but to make our shared experiences better. Welcome to the table. The first course we will share is the importance of centering in meditation and compassion. The only way to tap our power of inclusion is to be still and compassionate for all beings. The second course we will share is the importance of holding space to heal by listening. The power of inclusion requires that we listen deeply to our stories without judgment. Seeing life through the eyes of different experiences helps us transcend the edges of the pain we have carried through generations. The third course uplifts the leadership we need to succeed in being more diverse, equitable, accessible, and inclusive. The most important person we lead is ourselves. We are not merely the change we seek, but we are the only catalyst that can manifest the new day we long to see.

*Here is a moment to draw upon the breath
that connects us all.
Breathe deeply.
As you inhale, witness the pure energy of love,
flowing into the lungs of everyone,
regardless of their racialized body,
sexual expression, age, ability,
or any other aspect of how they show up in life.
As you exhale, send the compassion
of giving rather than receiving.
Savor your connection.
Allow your mind, heart, and spirit to say "welcome."*

CECILIA B. LOVING

Welcoming Begins with the Ability to Love Ourselves

Can you look into a mirror and say, "I love you"? It is not easy to do. The face I see sometimes is not the face I imagine. When I awaken or prepare for sleep, my mirror does not reflect make-up, hairdo, or coordinated clothing. *Who is that person?* I ask myself, realizing I am more than who I see. The superficiality is even more apparent when we work remotely. When no one else is around except my husband Marlon, I wear my glasses, work-out clothes, and no makeup, hair color, or style. I prioritize projects over-grooming unless I am required to be "camera-ready." Facing a mirror without the façade opens my eyes to who I am, beyond appearances. We are greater than who we appear to be in the flesh. We are so much more than our bodies. Staring back in the mirror are also our souls.

We begin to recognize the power of inclusion when we realize the soul's potential expressing as us, always tapping an aspect of ourselves to give to others. What we are here to share is far greater than what we see in a mirror. We support. We appreciate. We open our hearts to welcome, and by so doing, we experience the best of who we are. "Including" or treating others well is essential to our well-being.

Perhaps I did not see you because I am racialized as Black, or you did not see me because you are in a body racialized as White. Perhaps we did not see others because we assumed that they had nothing in common with us. Whatever differences we were taught or perceive are constructs. The construct that drives the greatest divide is race. Race is a significant edge to surpass to realize our innate ability to welcome or even be welcomed. The irony is that our health and well-being depend, even thrives, on supportive connections with everyone.

As the South African Zulu say, "Umuntu ngumuntu ngabantu," a person is a person through other people. "Ubuntu." I am because you are. I am here because of you, and you are here because of me. My heart and your heart are old friends. We are the fabric of a quilt of infinity that keeps adding eternal patches beyond who we appear to be in the physical. Me being here for you and you being here for me really is fundamental to our well-being.

We come from the womb realizing our oneness through the power of love, a pure power that resonates from our souls. But we are distracted by physical appearances. We notice the differences in our bodies rather than feel the oneness of our Spirit. We forget the indigenous teachings of our ancestors and adopt the greed of colonizers. Instead of realizing that there is enough, we believe in lack, that we can survive only by taking from someone else. Only a sincere welcome invites our souls to remember that we are one. Welcoming someone without fear or a calculated motive is one of the most important gifts you can give to the world.

Hopefully, we will live to see a time when we no longer need to expend our energy responding to an assault rather than a welcome. While we have done an amazing job of co-creating material things that make us feel safe and secure, we have not healed the trauma that lies in our bodies from past failures to embrace all humanity as one. Authentic, appreciative, and adaptive leadership are qualities that we must embody. We must ask and begin to answer the question posed by the person in the mirror. *Who are you? What are you here to give so that this world will be a better place?*

The world welcomed me with each breath that my new body took one Saturday in Detroit. I tried to come into this existence so fast that my mother almost gave birth to me at home. "Welcome," the universe breathed into me, a spiritual being having a human experience. Welcome, the civil rights movement of the '60s smiled at me. Welcome to the body of creation that summoned you into being. Welcome to the "ball of confusion" when all have forgotten that everyone is kin.

A Buddhist koan asks, do you remember what your parents' faces looked like before they were born? Yes, I remember: they were the faces of everyone, everywhere, always present. They were the gift of the thread of life connecting each being to one another so that we would not forget our oneness.

The body my soul chose is "racialized" as Black. I love being who I am. We often focus on the trauma but not the strength of our ancestors who gave birth to Black people in a world of hatred. I am grateful to be in the body of an African American female, born in a housing project in Detroit, to a family who showered me with love and thus taught me to be loving. I am glad my mother, who studied sewing with Rosa Parks, never really learned to sew but learned instead about civil rights. She taught us to learn our history and stay focused on the fight against injustice as soon as we entered the world.

Not having an abundance of material things provided a humble and compassionate lens through which to view the world. We were expected to be proud of our ethnicity. We were expected to be generous in supporting one another. We were expected to be strong, work hard, and put forth more than the concerted effort. We were expected to continue the struggle of bringing others to the table, supporting them once they got there, and giving them the opportunities that we never had with the welcome of all who come before us. We were expected to know that welcome does not just mean "come" and "be well" but demands that we give each other even more than we expect to receive.

Diversity, equity, accessibility, and inclusion ("DEAI") demand our dedication and commitment to those in our midst who we have an opportunity to welcome. We are not on this planet simply to grow up, educate ourselves, find work, have a family, and then die. We are all called to give our best to the world, which means uplifting the potential of one another.

*Here is a pause to consider whether you
have taken up the banner of Moses,
Harriet, Sojourner, Gandhi,
King, Mother Teresa, Douglas,
Bethune, Malcolm, Evers,
and so many others
who welcomed the souls of all humanity.
Breathe in the breath of their legacy,
welcoming those who are here,
and those yet to come.*

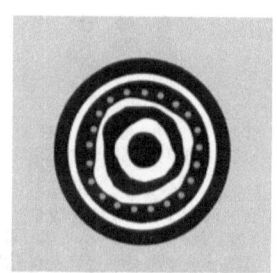

Welcoming is an Exercise of the Spirit

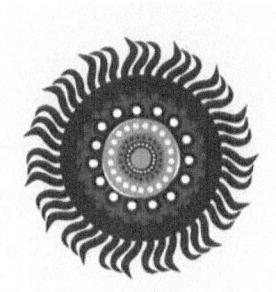

My mother's bedtime stories included the details of Kent State uprisings. My brothers and I read books about enslaved Africans and watched in Black and White as dogs and hoses attacked people striving for equality on television. Our library at home provided life-altering lessons in the fight that we are all born to continue: books by or about Harriet Tubman, Sojourner Truth, Booker T. Washington, George Carver, W.E.B. DuBois, James Baldwin, Richard Wright, Eldridge Cleaver, Franz Fanon, Dick Gregory, Ann Petry, Gwendolyn Brooks, Langston Hughes, and Ralph Ellison, to name a few who taught us the importance of the bodies that we were born in.

We welcomed the power of Spirit through history, the arts, education, and the church. None of our heroes would have triumphed without Spirit. They never acted alone, but with the force, energy, awareness, and grace that guided them to strive harder, love deeper, and be better. We were taught not to trust everyone but *never* to hate.

The Spirit that I speak of is in the church, synagogue, mosque, and temple but is not limited to holy places, worship, ancient text, or even religion. As Gandhi said, I am a Christian, a Muslim, a

Hindu, and a Jew. Spirituality, whose Latin origin means breath or breathe, transcends religion to include everyone. All beings, everywhere present, are united by the Spirit that makes us one. Another name for Spirit is love.

Love is everywhere present, always guiding us without condition. Like the time my mother told my four brothers and me that she would give ten dollars to anyone who could guess the name of her two hugging stuffed animals. After a quick meditation of silence in the bathroom, I returned and simply said, "Love and Happiness." *How did you know that?!* She demanded to know, but she understood that with Spirit, we are always guided to know what we need to know when we need to know it.

One time, I was even spiritually guided to look in a random pile of books in my basement, then through a box, next to open one nondescript hard copy book, which I opened and read. It not only had the lessons I received in my class, but I learned by studying it that it also contained the exams the teacher used because she did not choose to create her own. *What led me there?* There was nothing in the flesh that guided me to that box in a dimly lit basement piled with lots of boxes that I rarely opened.

I once dreamed every single detail of an experience I would have when I arrived at Howard University one summer, including a premature arrival, a mix-up in housing, various visits with people I knew, and an extended visit with the person who would come to my rescue. Each segment of my dream later took place, so I was guided to protect myself and knew who would ultimately welcome me in.

When I was in seminary, I completed projects on time because I could open a book and turn right to the page I needed. I worked full-time as a litigator but graduated first in my seminary class, giving help to whoever needed it. What we give gives back. I took seriously the charge that our ministry began in our classroom.

If we listen to Spirit, we will receive the guidance we need. Life beckons us not for ourselves but for others. The gift of giving returns in the form of even greater good. How can you reap the benefit of the good that the universe is conspiring to give you if you do not welcome it? Good shows up through other people. One of my colleagues, Wendy Star, has the gift of welcoming: a warm smile, a supportive presence, a kind heart, a loving disposition. She role-models welcoming others as an invitation to our own blessings. Our good may knock in the guise of a stranger, requiring that we give our hospitality even before developing trust. Welcoming can sometimes be uncomfortable, but we have the power to let good in by giving our best to each other. When we are welcoming to ourselves and others, the universe re-pays us in infinite ways.

Welcome.

Pause in the breath of your story.

*Welcome the awareness
of your birth, your childhood,
your education and service,
your work experience.*

Breathe out appreciation for all that you have given.

*What experience made you aware of
just how great you are?
What challenge gave you the fortitude
to be a resource for others?*

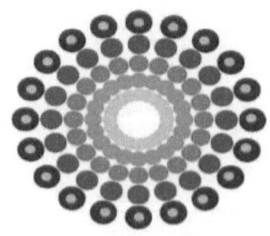

Welcoming Demands That We Cherish Ourselves

There is no question that those not racialized as Black need to be more welcoming to Black people. With such a high rate of bias against Black people, as shown by the Implicit Bias Test, around 90% of the world needs to be less biased against those racialized as Black. We need to appreciate and empower Black people and eliminate the false construct that Black people are less than (a falsehood carefully crafted by White people who wanted to justify terrorism and violence against Black people under the guise of slavery). One of the most traumatic results of being marginalized and denigrated is the impact on Black people's willingness to uplift and support ourselves.

If we cannot welcome ourselves, we do not have the capacity to welcome other people. If Black people don't love themselves, they will not have the capacity to love other Black people. We have all harmed and been harmed by not being welcomed. Some of the mistreatment that I have witnessed has also been perpetrated by Black people attacking other Black people through words, deeds, shame, blame, and humiliation.

We must check our racist tendencies in a racist world regardless of who we are or what we have accomplished. I have witnessed Black people who have made a lot of strides for other Black people still harbor racist beliefs and perpetuate the harm they suffered against other Black people. This cycle of self-abuse through generations is something that we fail to discuss. Nearly 50% of Black people harbor bias against each other, according to [the Implicit Bias Test](#).

In the same manner, women mistreat each other through competition, jealousy, and vindictiveness. Growing up in a family of boys, I never realized how jealous women could be of each other, failing to welcome each other with full appreciation rather than the pettiness of comparison.

One of the scars of oppression is not celebrating oneself and the talent of those who have been oppressed. The power of inclusion seizes the opportunity as victory to champion the disenfranchised as much as possible. How can I uplift your greatness should be the first question we ask ourselves on behalf of our BIPOC community. Failing to champion ourselves and each other undermines the core of our existence. We need to stop shouting "I'm not worthy" in church worship and gospel songs. Yes, you are worthy. Yes, you are good enough. Yes, you are amazing. As my friend Yomi reminds us: the sheer joy of our existence is something no one can take away.

As many of us in the Black community say in private: everyone helps their communities but us. The other thing we say behind closed doors is that no one needs to try to destroy us; we do that quite well ourselves. We need to welcome each other with the same warmth, appreciation, and acceptance we say we need from everyone else.

We can be proactive about letting others "know that we see them, hear them, and care about them" by creating opportunities to express appreciation through meetings, conversations, electronic communications, and day-to-day interactions. Welcoming requires unconditional acceptance of cultural and ethnic differences. We should also welcome everyone with a heart of genuine support, accepting them right where they are, with all of their unique attributes. When we do so, we find that the best we can bring to any relationship is free.

I am reminded of trips to museums, libraries, and other free experiences in art and theater that were always appreciated because my mother knew how to do a lot with a little. Mom knew how to create the best picnics and parties using more creativity than money. Similarly, one of Marlon's favorite memories is when his father created sleds out of huge boxes. When we appreciate ourselves and embrace who we are regardless of material things, we build the capacity to welcome others and share experiences with genuine appreciation and acceptance. We learn how to appreciate our communications and the relationships forged from them: the shared talk, the long walk, the potluck, the held hand, the cards given, the prayers expressed, the simple act of being present for one another.

We give the greatest gift there is with our presence, and by so doing, we increase our ability to give who we are instead of what we can buy. What we give of ourselves returns. We might even see that those we welcome actually mirror our own behavior.

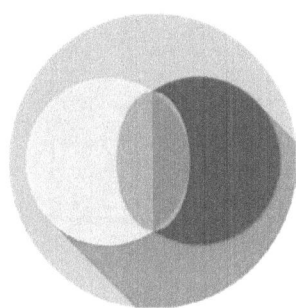

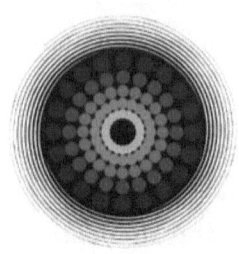

*Take a moment and breathe the power of connecting
with those who look like you,
as well as those who don't.
Allow yourself to relax in the moment.
Think about a person or group of people
different than you
Open your heart to welcome them.
Reach out to someone you never spend time with,
and listen to their story. Walk with them.
Sit with them. Welcome them.
Spend several minutes breathing in
and breathing out gratitude, joy, and support for them.
Bless whatever challenges are on their path.*

• CHAPTER 2 •

Honor

*When we find our purpose,
our calling to contribute our lives to others,
we embrace a movement,
to serve others in an inclusive way.*

When I was growing up, my mother used to say, "if people would just mind their own business, everything would be alright." One of the most important questions we can ask ourselves is, "what *is* my business?" What is my purpose? Why am I here right now? What was I called to do? Why am I living, breathing, and taking up space? Only an understanding of our purpose here and now in this life will enable us to serve others in the most inclusive manner possible. When we discern our purpose and dedicate our lives to a cause greater than ourselves, a cause that serves other people, we find our purpose in life as well as the greatest fulfillment that there is.

DEAI was always my purpose. When I was born, however, there was not a field called DEAI. Over time, we realized that the need that we share to be accountable and uplift one another is a full-time occupation. Now, we know it is even more; it is a shared responsibility. We will honor new careers, callings, and passions in time, creating names for them, titles, certifications, and even degrees. As long as we honor what we are here to do, an opportunity to do the work will manifest itself. When I was studying theater, production, business, law, and then ministry, I had no idea that it would provide a strong foundation for working in the DEAI space.

We must honor our purpose regardless of what it is: whether we are preventing or responding to fires and other emergencies; making our streets, parks, transportation, schools, and neighborhoods safe; delivering or selling what we need; teaching, guiding and caring for our children; sewing, scrubbing, fixing and building; nursing, doctoring, or otherwise caring for the elderly, sick, shut-in, deceased, or disabled; praying, ministering, counseling, healing, or leading, our government, corporations and other businesses; representing those who seek justice or must defend themselves; manufacturing, farming, building, growing, or cultivating the things we need; driving, designing, innovating, and creating outside of the boxes that can no longer contain us.

Honoring our purpose requires no explanation.

It does not matter whether others cannot understand our purpose or what others think of us: what matters is whether we believe in ourselves.

Here is a space to pause in honor of your calling,
a moment to remember your breath
and honor your life's purpose.

Close your eyes, or leave them slightly open,
and connect with the breath, here and now.
Quietly ask yourself
"Why am I here in this experience, at this time?
What is my purpose?"
Take a moment and think about it.
Write in a journal or on a note to yourself
whatever comes up for you.

What do you enjoy doing the most for others?
What would you do for free?
What would you do if money were no object?

CECILIA B. LOVING

We Are Here to Serve Something Greater Than Ourselves

In 1993, I was in the World Trade Center when it was bombed. One of my colleagues and I walked down 86 flights to leave the building as firefighters climbed up those flights. On the days immediately after 9/11, I knew that my calling was to serve a power greater than the world, and I opened my Bible to reach beyond the destruction around me to the protective energy of spiritual love. Faith was the only solace that I felt. No one anywhere should suffer. As 17th-century poet-saint Rahman Baba wrote, "We are all one body. Whoever tortures another, wounds himself." These words apply to everyone.

We love a garden because of its many different flowers and fragrances, shapes, and colors. Science shows that our diversity is beneficial to our work. Our differences exist to create more beauty, power, and strength. Our differences teach us that we are love for all things, all beings, all expressions of faith. Experts have already proven that diversity brings in more profitability and greater innovation. DEAI is a "no brainer." Yet, we stand in the way of its success.

When I saw those firefighters running up endless flights of stairs, I understood the honor of serving something greater than who I am. What a metaphor to be able to rise in the potential of something greater than fear. May we rise in the strength of those who came before us. May we bless the past and know that we built this country on the aspiration of the liberty and justice of infinite possibilities and endless opportunities for everyone. May we plant new seeds of courage and a lasting consciousness of change to fortify the faith that brought us this far.

We arrive in this existence with so many different experiences, throughout so many different phases of growth, immersed in so many different truths, tribes, testimonies, and tongues that we forget that just as much as we are different, we are the same. We are born. We covet. We doubt. We sin. We fall. We fear. We wander. We desire. We complain. We regress. We bless. We imagine. We surrender. We realize that we are much more than the breath of creation. Each one of us is a gift. Our accomplishments are mere guideposts, benchmarks to show us the ultimate gift: we are here to give, and by so giving—to serve, and by so serving—to be our best.

There is no quick fix to properly perform "inclusion," locate the root cause of exclusion, address it, and return for an after-action debriefing of the entire operation. The challenges that we face to be more inclusive will not change overnight, during a single run or exercise, nor can they be obliterated by a course. Success in DEAI is not based on the mere accomplishment of initiatives but also on the fundamental commitment to lead and exemplify the acceptance, respect, and value of everyone. Each accomplishment in DEAI makes us aware of even more work to be done.

True power is not indicative of how we rule, govern, or assert strength over someone else but how we demonstrate an ability to uplift our own gifts, as well as the talents of others. Everything around us teaches us that we cannot remain in the past any more than we can remain in a burning building. The message of the pandemic is that we must be better. We are safe in our families, safe in our tribes, safe in our communities, and safe in the world because we are in tune with who we are and because we are one with those around us.

As Fire Chief Malcolm Moore says, "each day I go to work uplifted by the fact that I will be a blessing to somebody who may be experiencing the worse day of their life." Our purpose is not simply for us. We are here to serve something greater than ourselves: that prophetic call felt in our minds, hearts, and souls before we were formed in the womb is the most powerful aspect of our being. Our callings will summon us. We do not need to look hard for our purpose, but we must honor it once found. In so doing, we honor others, as well as ourselves.

Your purpose says, "you got this," even when your inner critic (and we all have an inner critic or negativity bias) tries to doubt you. When you know what your calling is, neither haters nor naysayers can de-rail you from your purpose. When you adhere to your purpose, your good will unfold. The universe will take whatever obstacles threaten you and use them as a catalyst to bless you in accordance with your purpose. No matter what, discern and stay connected to your purpose.

Regardless of how we express our individual goals and desires, our purpose is the way we express our love for life and for others.

In other words, our calling or greater purpose is not merely to satisfy our egos but exists to give from the guidance of Spirit. Our purpose is a call to respond to the truth that is both an individual passion and communal need to support everyone.

To honor your purpose, you must not merely hear your calling but also respond to it. The work that we do is not merely to make money or feed our personal ambition. What we give our lives to do is not about us but about those we serve.

We are here to contribute to the well-being of those around us, which is what inclusion is all about. Inclusion is not merely a lofty workplace goal but a mindset that will enhance our own well-being by allowing us to carry out our purpose in life. We love where we work when it allows us to do what we are passionate about doing.

We cultivate a deeper connection to community when we center on our purpose. This requires us to be calm, relaxed, and focused, which is achieved in the silence. Aligning our purpose with our values helps us minimize the negative thoughts that often come up for us. When we focus on the bigger picture, we can choose our battles and not give our energy to a distraction, something, or someone who does not support our greater purpose.

Take a moment to think about your core values.
What has brought you to where you are today?
Have your experiences provided you with opportunities
to assist others?
Does your purpose reflect or otherwise support your core values?

Your core values are a roadmap to understanding your purpose.
Take a moment and think about your core values.
Do they align with your greater purpose in life?
How do you cultivate better alignment with your purpose and
through that awareness give to the world?

Breathe in the awareness of what you have done
and/or what you should do.

Using Meditation to Cultivate Purpose

Meditation or mindfulness, the practice of focusing on the present moment without judgment, is important for honoring purpose because when we are centered in meditation, we are more in tune with the guidance of Spirit, to what I call the divine ideas that are always available to us. Stress, worry, and doubt put us in a survival mode that is not conducive to creativity. Purpose helps us stay centered. When we align with purpose, we are not self-indulgent; we shift our perspective from "me" to "we."

If we feel threatened, we go into a lower state of consciousness, shutting down and fighting for survival rather than creating. Meditation helps move beyond the "fight, flight, or freeze" reaction of a lower state of consciousness and supports a growth mindset, which allows us to be proactive rather than merely react. With meditation, we develop a growth mindset instead of a fixed mindset. A fixed mindset is rigid and afraid to move beyond limited thinking.

I was called into the ministry while practicing law and had no idea what a ministerial calling would entail. But I knew that I had to be obedient. After finishing seminary, I spent ten years leading a church each Sunday with very few people because the church offered a traditional forum to respond to my calling. Our callings, however, do not always express themselves in traditional ways. I was ordained to bring spirituality to the workplace, but I had no idea what that looked like in 2007. I would meditate and pray regarding my "purpose" and leave it to the guidance of a force greater than me. I would say to myself, "I am open to doing whatever you want me to do, God."

For nearly 10 years, Marlon and I, along with several of our church members, would meet at the Unity Center of New York Center, where we meditated together, prayed together, sang together, and visualized together. I shared a lesson via PowerPoint, during which I entertained questions each Sunday. Whether my church community would grow enough to sustain the physical structure of a church home and parish type community was a critical question because otherwise, it would not sustain Sunday services on a long-term basis. Gratefully, we began to use technology early on through live-streaming on truthunity.net and video conferencing, as well as a virtual prayer call and an online meditation. We have held virtual meditation practices now for almost ten years. In 2018, we created a free APP, SPIRITMUV CHURCH-IN-MOTION, to access meditation and lessons online.

But I was ordained to bring spirituality to the workplace. *What does that look like?* I wondered. How would that take shape when I did not believe in proselytizing or trying to convert others to my faith. I don't believe in force-feeding religion or similar beliefs or philosophies. If you are reading the *Power of Inclusion*, it is because you chose to read it. When the student is ready, the teacher appears; when the teacher is ready, the student is there.

My calling was in the workplace, so I had to trust Spirit to guide me to its unfoldment. I went back to work while I continued to hold Sunday services, do workshops, bible studies, retreats, prayer calls, build websites, and do daily meditation practices online. At one point, I had to decide on a job, and I meditated over it. When I came out of the meditation, I was led to work at the NYC Commission on Human Rights, which I now realize was a critical decision on the path to responding to my calling. Understanding Human Rights is important to our work in DEAI.

I had always been committed to diversity and inclusion in the workplace, but I never thought of its spiritual implications until I was appointed Chief Diversity and Inclusion Officer at the Fire Department of New York City. My mandate was to provide leadership in creating a "positive and holistic" work environment. As soon as I was in the role, I realized that leading DEAI was my true calling and ministry. Not only is God defined in the Holy Bible as "love," but the greatest commandment is to love one another.

"Inclusion" is just another name for love.

If we use love as a catalyst, we can accept and celebrate everyone.

Everything I did for my church prepared me for the work I needed to do to be a thought leader in DEAI. Every Sunday for years, I spoke to a discerning audience invited to raise questions, encouraging debate and reflection. I prepared presentations each week. I created, lead, and guided meditations, retreats, and workshops. I published books and articles in all mediums, created messaging through websites, blogs and videos. I counseled, led, and guided through "healing" circles. Looking back, I realize that meditation revealed my calling, showed me my purpose, and guided me every step of the way.

*Some say that our purpose is shaped
before we are formed in the womb.
Even if we are not aware of it,
our purpose is always inside of us,
just waiting for our discovery.*

*Take a moment and breathe in an awareness
of connection to your purpose.*

*Center in the joy of what you love to do.
Feel the commitment and the satisfaction
of oneness with your purpose,
always uplifting you
with how great it feels to bless others
by doing what you love to do,
regardless of recognition or reward.*

Our Soul is Our Guide

Our purpose influences the course of our lives and is made even more apparent if we are open and receptive to it. Our soul, which is already tuned into our purpose, guides us to greater awareness.

I love what Browne Landone says in *Soul Catalysts*: our souls are not in our bodies; they are too enormous to be contained by mere flesh; no, we are in our souls. Sometimes the soul guides us to more challenging situations to grow and stretch beyond our comfort zones. The soul aligns our purpose with the opportunities that we need to better serve it. We can trust that the soul, which is more in tune with Divine Mind (or whatever you call the Quantum Realm, Spirit, or God), is tapped into the synergy needed to carry out our purpose.

You never know where your good is coming from. It might be from someone you do not really like, or from a friend. It might be from a stranger or from someone you know well. Your greatest good, in alignment with your purpose, might even come from someone you are biased against, and the mere fact that you cannot honor them will block you from honoring your purpose.

Some say the soul knows all. I agree that the soul knows what we need before we even ask. The way we align with our soul's purpose more easily is to use the energy of love, sending love and being loving to everyone you meet, even those difficult to love. By doing so, you don't block your good, which can come from anywhere or anyone.

Inclusion fuels the energy that we need to be our best and be open and receptive to the infinite gifts shared by those who may be different. When we are open and inclusive, our purpose will reveal itself. A career is not necessarily a purpose unless we are paid to do what we love to do. If our jobs fully align with our purpose, then we know that we have honored our calling through our careers.

When I think about callings, one person who comes to mind is Pete Souza, the photographer for Presidents Reagan and Obama. He talked about a book that he had of the White House as a child and how often he sat with it and looked at its photographs. His story is fully aligned with purpose. Souza became a photographer, even though his mother was not pleased that he would do what appeared to be a frivolous thing in her eyes after he obtained a college degree. But Souza honored his passion, and sure enough, he returned full circle to the book he treasured as a child by writing his own book of photography entitled *Shade*. The book of photos he loved as a child was really his soul calling him to his purpose.

On my proverbial death bed at 18 years old, I awoke one spring morning in April at Harper Hospital in Detroit, down to 77 lbs., and what I call Spirit said, "you will live to write." I write, but I know that it is one aspect of responding to my calling. Writing is also messaging, communicating, and storytelling—all of which are important to the ministry of inclusion.

There are over 400 billion planets where many different life forms exist, so improving our consciousness to be more kind and loving towards each other is the bare minimum. How can we effectively engage with a universe of galaxies and beings who don't look, think, breed, eat, or communicate like humans if we cannot first accept ourselves? Loving each other is a baby step that is part of our evolution to begin the journey that expands our consciousness to meet the future that awaits us.

In Tim Kelley's *True Purpose*, he says, "egos and souls do not speak the same 'language.' Egos tend to divide things into groups, to categorize and judge them. Souls do not." Purpose is not about collecting people, increasing those we control, making the most money, obtaining the most awards or accomplishments, or even writing the most books; it is about giving our heart to the betterment of all with honor and humility.

Honor can be scary. We have no idea where our purpose will lead us, but we can trust that the soul guides us in perfect divine order. If we could see where we need to be before we were ready, we would probably run in the opposite direction, second-guessing our divine nature and infinite wisdom. If we looked before we leaped, we would be susceptible to those nagging inner critics who say we don't have what it takes. The soul helps us stop standing in our own way, realizing that the net will appear whenever we leap.

How do we know that we are honoring our purpose? We know that we are passionate, energetic, synchronized, perhaps even giddy in anticipation of opportunities to do the work we are called to do. When we are in synch with our calling, we feel the flow and synergy of perfect, divine order.

*Take a moment and pause in the synergy
that brought you to this moment.
Feel gratitude for every situation
that brought you to this space of appreciation.
Create a list of situations that you can be thankful for.
Send gratitude to everyone who comes to your mind.
Send an email, text, or note to someone of another background,
culture, or religion, preferably someone to whom you have
never given thanks and who has impacted
your honor and commitment to purpose.*

THE POWER OF INCLUSION

Purpose Enhances Trust

Harriet Tubman trusted her ability to rescue hundreds of enslaved Africans because she understood her purpose. She escaped enslavement herself and risked being recaptured, beaten, and killed when she returned, again and again, to help hundreds of Africans escape slavery in this country. Her courage and strength indicate her faith in God's power and a deep connection to her purpose.

During one mission in a bitter snowstorm, she found that the enslaved Africans she intended to help escape were not at their appointed meeting place. She did not turn back because she only had a tree for shelter. She did not refuse to wait in the storm. Trusting her divine purpose, she stood behind the tree for the entire night in a snowstorm until those she came to help arrived.

The abolitionists who wrote this account depicted her as an ignorant child instead of a powerful Spirit woman and called "her people's" trust in God naive. But Tubman's trust is why we still recognize her courage, tenacity, strength, and resilience today. Despite the death-defeating odds, she was not afraid to risk her life each day to help hundreds escape the indignity and horror of American slavery.

When we realize our greater calling, core values, and how they inform our purpose in life, we move beyond the limits of fear to serve a far greater cause than us and our personal issues. We trust when we know that we are on the right path. We trust that our purpose is aligned with our values. Then, no matter what happens, our values align with our purpose. Being aware of our purpose is fundamental to being inclusive. Being committed to our purpose is also imperative to our health and well-being.

One way of centering on your values and purpose is to create a leadership philosophy. My values align with my leadership philosophy, which guides my purpose, expressed through the acronym **INCLUSIVE:**

> I – INCLUSIVE - welcoming everyone
> N – NETWORK - nurturing connection
> C – CREATIVITY - innovating ideas
> L – LOVE - giving unconditionally
> U – UNWAVERING - remaining determined
> S – SAFETY - supporting growth
> I – INTEGRITY - staying honest
> V – VICTORIOUS - seizing success
> E – EMOTIONAL INTELLIGENCE - honoring others

Pause in the power of your purpose.
Take a moment right now and breathe with honor.
Follow in gratitude with your hand over your heart,
with thanks for your
commitment to your purpose.

Feel the power of your soul,
in which you live, and move,
and have your being.

Connect with love guiding you.

What are your core values?
Take a moment,
and think about five to ten
values that are important to you.

Take the time to journal
why they are important to you,
and how these values inform your purpose in life.

*How can you incorporate your values
with how you lead your life,
as well as how you lead others
into a leadership philosophy?*

*Is there a word that best describes you,
which can incorporate
all of your core values?*

*What is your brand?
What makes you exceptionally you?
What brings you joy when you share
your gifts and talents?*

*What should you release that
no longer serves the greater
vision of who you are?*

*How can you stretch in
and grow in the power of your purpose?*

CHAPTER 3

Meditate

Inclusion finds power in the stillness
of simply being,
slowing down to experience the
greatest love that is and ever will be.

The most important thing that we can do for ourselves, which is the core of being more inclusive of others, is to find the stillness within and in that stillness, to simply be one with the moment. The ability to be our best self requires that we go within, calming the external noise and distractions, and finding that reservoir of power that ignites our spirit. Inclusion begins within. If we cannot connect with the core of who we are, we will lack the fortitude to fight for anything, much less fight for justice. If we cannot find peace within, we will have difficulty being peaceful. Whatever we want to express on the outside, we must first find on the inside.

The Inclusion of Silence

Activism is not just what we do but who we are and how we show up for ourselves and others. Inclusion requires mindfulness, but the mere practice of mindfulness does not make you inclusive. The simplest form of mindfulness is sometimes the most difficult, simply being silent and paying attention to the breath. Each day, we need time to be quiet and listen to the stillness. For us born in a culture of expressing worship more outwardly, through hymns, creeds, communion, tongues, or the Holy Ghost, this may be a new concept, but it is one to include in our arsenal of Spirit. Being still is a practice that supports inclusion because it helps reduce implicit bias, calm the mind, and make us less judgmental. When we are still, we not only help others, we also help ourselves.

When we listen in silence, every part of us hears. We hear the inner guidance that is always informing us. When we slow down and listen, we rise above the fray; as Einstein would say, *we need to solve our problems at a different level than that which created them in the first place.*

The good thing about mindfulness is that it can be talked about in the workplace as non-religious. It offers a secular practice that affords us the ability to be silent together without the bias for or against a particular faith. No one owns the stillness. It invites all of us to center daily and breathe awareness, connection, and trust.

Since I began meditating as part of my spiritual practice around 1974, meditation remains an essential part of my faith. We, however, can remove religious references from meditation so that the practices are more welcoming to those who do not share religious beliefs. Meditation is important in maintaining focus, providing one of the best tools for resilience, and enhancing compassion, kindness, and appreciation.

Mindfulness is one form of meditation, defined as being aware of the present moment without judgment, but I don't limit mindfulness to a particular definition. I like the broad definition of mindfulness that Sharon Salzberg provides and its depth for release and openness. She says, "mindfulness is the practice of paying attention in a way that creates space for insight."

For me, mindfulness includes the rhythms, spirituals, blues, drums, and beats that liberate me, like those liberating Radha Blank in *The 40th Year Old Version* on Netflix. Her unique expression was her greatest gift. In my "baptized imagination," I submit that the first meditations were part of the daily existence of the earliest humans born in Africa. All indigenous people rely on the intuitive connection that we experience through mindfulness.

Because of my roots in womanist theology (how Black women walk and talk with God), I define mindfulness as finding a connection with love, and yet, a definition cannot contain mindfulness. Mindfulness should be free to step outside of the box of convention and mold, shape, and contort into infinite expressions that will change whenever anyone practices it. A White male Buddhist from Scarsdale will likely practice mindfulness in a much different way than a Black female Baptist from Detroit. But what centers us in the present moment "without judgment" is for us to determine for ourselves.

In the ancient text, Jesus shares many important moments that were part of his practice of mindfulness. For example, in John 14:20, Jesus provides the following contemplative meditation:

"I am in my Father, and you [are] in Me, and I [am] in you."

For me, each sentence that Jesus speaks is a meditation. Here, He opens wide the space of our connection, that there is no separation between us and all that we worship. This is the ultimate meditation, the simple realization that we are one.

Some might choose to meditate on a Buddhist koan, hold a yoga pose, or breathe the deep compassion of tonglen. Sometimes I choose those things too. Let us uplift all the sacred texts, the Sutras, the Bible, the Vedas, the Qur'an, the Gita, the Torah, the Guru Granth Sahib, the Tripitaka, and all sources of spiritual inspiration as powerful sources of centering. As the Buddhist monk Thích Nhât Hanh once said, "some Christians are more Buddhist than Buddhists, and some Buddhists are more Christian than Christians."

One of my spiritual gurus is [Sharon Salzberg](#) because she embodies love in all that she is through the power of mindfulness. The gospel that resonates through her teachings, retreats, and books is love, "real love" she teaches, supporting "real change," not romanticism. We don't like to say "love" so much in the workplace. Yet, love and support for others are what inclusion is all about.

Without love, you can have a daily practice of mindfulness and still be racist. Without love, you can do the work that you believe levels the playing ground for others or be committed to hiring diverse people but still be racist. Love is the foundation of meditation. A practice devoid of love is inherently racist because it lacks the capacity that Dr. Ibram X. Kendi uplifts to be proactive about including others. Mindfulness without compassion is meaningless.

Take a moment right now and breathe
in compassion for everyone
regardless of their differences.
Allow yourself to relax in the moment.
Use the opportunity to send healing thoughts
of love throughout the entire planet.

CECILIA B. LOVING

Meditation as Prayer

Meditation is not a religion, but we can choose to incorporate it into every aspect of our lives: our health and well-being, our family and personal relationships, our work and career development, our world view and community, and also our religion and faith. I incorporate meditation in everything that I do, as Brother Lawrence and Thích Nhât Hanh would say, practicing the presence. For example, every Saturday morning, at 7:00 A.M., I hold a circle of prayer. The circle originated from a 40-day prayer circle I held after Easter 2014 to pay tribute to the power of the resurrection of Jesus. We always focus on the crucifixion but rarely do we consider the teachings that Jesus imparted the 40 days before the ascension. Our prayers intensified during the pandemic, when we finished 100 consecutive days of prayer, as shared in my book *Good Medicine: 100 Prayers From the Pandemic*. We continue to come together to pray every Saturday in whatever form or shape our prayers take: words, thoughts, silence, presence, awareness, a circle embodying the pure energy of love, as well as mindfulness meditation practices. Our prayer circle creates a space for insight.

THE POWER OF INCLUSION

As our practice deepens, we become aware that the gathering itself is our meditation. We are guided through meditation rather than asking for things. In the breath of a single moment, we realize that we don't have to beg because our miracles are here. The pure presence and power of perfect health and wholeness are here.

When we are open to the pure consciousness of love expressing as us, we find an altar right in our souls. We can listen to our own breath and be restored. Listening to the breath and being one with the moment is not merely resilience; it is grace.

We are not sinners who have to convince an old man in the sky of anything. Love already knows. Love looks, breathes, laughs, and dances with us as we breathe in and out in the peace of simply being. When we center on the breath that connects us all, we can slow down and be aware of everyone and everything without judgment. We can approach the altar of forgiveness with unconditional compassion and spare no one the power of love emanating from our hearts.

What would we ask of the love that is our own being, whose blessings line every cell, molecule, atom, and aspect of who we are? When we are still, we know that we have all that we need, and no one and nothing can deprive us of it. In this energy, we are inclusive because we recognize everyone who is and ever be in the stillness.

CECILIA B. LOVING

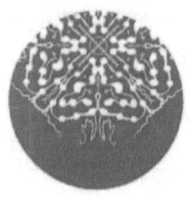

*Faith, regardless of which creed we choose,
is an essential part of our well-being.
Here is a moment to center in the
powerful energy of our faith.*

*Here is a moment to kneel within
at the altar of absolute good
and revel in how it has carved
ways out of no way,
and given us the courage
to succeed when nothing else could.*

*Here is an opportunity to breathe in the miracles
that surround us if we choose.
We are all given the power to bless each other,
and to start by blessing ourselves.*

Meditation and Implicit Bias

The science supports that we are all biased. No matter how positive we are, we all have a negativity bias. Lawyers, for example, suffer a great amount of internal negativity. Dr. Larry Richard, an expert on the psychology of lawyers and owner of a consulting group called LawyerBrain, says lawyers compound negativity because we are trained to be skeptical, always anticipate what could go wrong, and are hired to be adversarial. Lawyers suffer from high stress and low resilience and have a fixed rather than a growth mindset.

We all embody the historical trauma of our ancestors, who had internal alarms to respond to and protect ourselves from physical danger. Our history, experiences, family, education, environments, media, and many other elements also compound our internal alarms with the toxins of shame, blame, and guilt. Just as much as we are biased against others, we are also biased against ourselves. To compound our challenge further, our work environments are complex webs of social systems experienced by our brains as stressful, triggering the same defenses required in the harsh terrain thousands of years ago when surviving the attack of animals and the elements as hunter-gatherers. Therefore, we must recalibrate our internal alarm system to manage our inner trauma and create an inclusive mindset that is more positive than negative.

As previously mentioned, we measure biases through mechanisms like the Implicit Association Test (the "IAT") developed by Mahzarin Banaji and Anthony Greenwald. IAT data reveals that implicit bias is pervasive and approximately 75 percent of Americans display an implicit (automatic) preference for White people over Black people. Banaji and Greenwald establish that most discrimination against Black people is not explicit, overt prejudice but is implicit and is the primary contributor to the disadvantages experienced by Black people. The toxins of bias run so deep that we cannot reduce them unless we change our consciousness. One way to help reduce implicit bias is with meditation.

Several studies support the use of mindfulness to reduce implicit bias (*e.g.*, Yoona Kang, Jeremy Gray and John Dovidio (2013)(the "Kang Study"); Adam Lueke and Bryan Gibson (2014 and 2015)(the "Leuke/Gibson Studies"); and Alexander Stell and the University of Sussex (2015)(the "Stell Study"). In Yoona Kang's study, volunteers were assigned to one of three groups to measure their implicit bias against Black people and homeless people. One group practiced a lovingkindness meditation for six weeks; a second group discussed lovingkindness meditations without practicing them; a third group did not practice any meditations. At the end of the six weeks, the only group whose "implicit bias" against Black people and homeless people "significantly decreased" was the group who practiced the lovingkindness meditation. Just learning, thinking about, and discussing compassion and equality was not enough to change deep-rooted biases.

In the Stell Study, scientists found that participants who performed a seven-minute lovingkindness meditation practice with Black people as their focal point significantly diminished their bias against Black people. The Leuke/Gibson Studies showed that meditation in reducing bias does not need to be restricted to loving-kindness meditations. Participants in both studies engaged in 10 minutes of mindfulness meditation, which showed significantly less bias.

If we stop, take a moment, and pause to listen, not only are we more aware of our own thoughts and more intuitive to the situations around us, we also learn to be less judgmental, less critical, and even less biased of others. The pure potential of awareness begins when we realize that now is all that matters. When we focus on the inhalation and exhalation of each breath, we are better able to release our worries about the past and the future—and breathe new possibilities by being present without judgment.

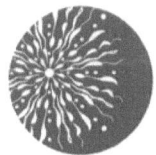

Breathe in and out an awareness of the healing power of love.
If we spend each day sending love to others throughout
the world, we would heal hatred
with the compassion of patience, gratitude,
and peace and a kind thought, a simple gesture,
a breath removing the brittleness of bias.

CECILIA B. LOVING

Practicing the Presence

My mother tells the story of how I laid out as a small child in the middle of our front yard and stared up with amazement at the clouds. She wondered what I was thinking. I have been meditating for as long as I can remember. One of the first books I recall reading was one that my mother borrowed from her friend Dessie in 1974: *Mind: The Master Power* by Charles Roth, published by Unity Books. I also had one called *Silence as Yoga* by Swami Paramananda. The silence was always something that appealed to me. I was born knowing that life was much greater than what we see in the flesh and that we need to be still to tap its full potential.

I spent almost 20 years listening to the live guided meditations of the late Olga Butterworth, wife of the late renowned Unity Minister Eric Butterworth, who would fill Lincoln Center in Manhattan every Sunday with people of all faiths meditating. We began and ended service with a guided meditation. Later, after both Eric and Olga made their transitions, I began holding my own services at the Unity Center, which also began and ended with a meditation.

Meditation is called a practice because we must practice it, and only through practice do we achieve results. We can begin by spending at least a few minutes a day in meditation. When we learn to settle our bodies and practice wise and compassionate self-care, our focus is not reducing stress but increasing our ability to manage stress, as well as about creating more room for our nervous system to find coherence and flow. For example, we can focus our attention on the center of our bellies, behind our navels. Breathe in and out, deeply and slowly, a few times. Pull the air all the way down into our bellies. Keep breathing, deeply and slowly. Follow our breath as it flows through our noses, throats, lungs, and bellies. Keep following it as it flows back out again.

Just meditating 15-30 minutes a day may help reverse the appearance of aging, improve our overall demeanor, as well as reduce our unconscious biases. It does not matter if we are introduced to mindfulness at the mosque, temple, church, dojo, revival, or on the job. The most important thing to do is practice it, and from that starting place, we eventually discover what works best for us. There are ample meditation applications, including but not limited to Journey Meditations; Stop, Breathe and Think; Headspace; Calm; and my own daily Mindfulness Blog, at https://mindfulnessgroup.blog/.

The onus to practice meditation consistently and to develop greater compassion is not the responsibility of some rather than others but what we all should do to better tap the power within. Those who have been oppressed in this country have long used the tools of meditation, prayer, devotionals, compassion, gratitude, singing, humming, shouting, and other practices to deal with the trauma of coping with racism and prejudice. Otherwise, we would not have survived the intense brutality of slavery, Jim Crow, lynching, police violence, and other forms of oppression. Practicing meditation does not make us less effective but more resilient in combatting injustice, strengthening ourselves to not only be courageous but to connect with a source greater than our physical experiences. Meditation is as free as the wind and the sky, always available to breathe through us.

*Take a moment and close your eyes,
and breathe three times,
keeping your thoughts only on your breath.*

*Breathing in, breathing out.
Breathing in, breathing out.
Breathing in, breathing out.*

*That awareness of being fully present
with the moment is the foundation
of all mindfulness practices.*

• CHAPTER 4 •

Listen

*Inclusion listens deeply,
beyond space and time,
with ears that hear through hearts,
eyes that see beyond judgment,
and souls that hold safe spaces.*

When King preached a vision of the community called "Beloved," he left to us to shape and mold its emergence. Listening is one of the most profound ways to build community and the only way to build a community of compassion. But listening is not easy. Most of us do not take the time to listen because it is so much easier to be consumed by the noise around us. But if we pause to listen, not only are we more aware of our own thoughts and more intuitive to the situation around us, we learn to be less judgmental, less critical, and even less biased of others.

Gina Leow, one of my colleagues and "reverse" mentors, is the best listener I know. I try to remember what she does when I am listening to someone else. She listens without her own agenda in mind. She is patient and never interrupts. She looks into your eyes without judgment, and you feel as though she genuinely wants to hear what you have to say. Another reverse mentor, Tameka Lowe, is also a fantastic listener, which she follows up with action. She listens with compassion, purpose, and attention and uses what she knows to facilitate change.

Listening is one of the greatest gifts we can give to someone. Being present for others as they share their story is one of the most important ways to acknowledge that someone else is valuable. Listening is how we show up and give our best without focusing on what we want in return. Most misunderstandings occur because we fail to listen without judgment. Listening is not space within which to create our own narrative or impose the judgments of others. Instead, listening is an opportunity for us to be fully present to the stories of others.

Perhaps you have something painful or difficult to share; I can help you heal that part of your suffering by listening. Maybe you want to tell me something that I'm afraid to hear because I believe that I am to blame for your suffering: listening opens up spaciousness that allows me to hold what is important to you and gives both of us the ability to heal. If I don't listen, I am left to my imagination, and we both continue to suffer.

Listening helps us say the words deep in our souls that need to be dislodged from our bellies and shared. Listening helps pull from our consciousness whatever troubles or even gives us joy. By speaking our words, we release our anxieties, our cares, our fears. Many White people are afraid to listen to the suffering of Black people because they believe they are the source and are guilty of the pain of generations of Black people born in a racist world. Listening is the first step towards healing. Similarly, many Black people don't want to listen to White people because they believe that White people are so oblivious to the pain that they cause that their ignorance is too painful to bear. Having a conversation where judgment interferes with our ability to hear is not listening.

When we cannot trust those we share our truth with, we will not have full communication. We will, then, not reveal too much, especially not to share those things that would make us vulnerable. True listening is a sacred contract that simply allows us to hear what is important to someone else without judgment or risk of condemnation, which helps to create a safe space. True listening allows us to share our imperfections, our shame, our crazy, our vulnerabilities—without worrying that what we share will make us less than or turn into something that can be used against us.

It's good to do listening dyads: exercises where two people take turns listening to each other and switch. The listening portion is timed: one minute, two minutes, or three minutes. The period is generally short because listening is difficult to do. We need to gradually increase the timing to press against our impatience and learn to be fully present for each session.

That's what I love about circles, which I discuss more fully in the next chapter. Everyone must be listened to, no matter how long it takes. While you listen to everyone's share and pass the talking piece, you realize that sometimes it is not our stories that heal us but the stories of others.

In a circle, you can only speak from your own experience. You touch the edges of your own pain and suffering, your own confusion and messiness, or perhaps even your own light and love. You are forced to listen. By the time the talking piece reaches you, you have opened a space within yourself that needed opening—only because you heard someone else's story.

Only through listening do we discover that what is important to someone else is different from what is important to us, or maybe it's the same. We learn that our thoughts are only one aspect of a myriad of differences. We learn that we have a gift to share that requires nothing monetary. We can cultivate spaces of giving and receiving that we never knew we had within us.

I met my friend Sabrina from a listening dyad that we participated in together at a conference. We had never met before, but we listened to each other. Now we celebrate birthdays and holidays together; we pray together, and we continue life's journey together in an important way because we shared an opportunity to listen.

Take a moment and look deeply into the eyes
of someone else and listen.
Through our listening, we see them, and
realize the importance of being aware.

II.

HEALING WITH GENEROSITY

When we learn
that there is no "them"
but only "us"
and that when one being hurts,
we are all harmed,
we will begin
the deep inner work
that it takes to heal.

• CHAPTER 5 •

Circle

*Inclusion forms a circle
where two or more gather
as beating hearts listen,
talking pieces pass,
and stories witness healing
all parts of ourselves.*

I heard my mother's words, "let the circle be unbroken," long before I knew I was a Circle Keeper. Now, I realize that restorative circles are among the most powerful tools available to help create a more positive and holistic world. Circles open communication channels, help resolve conflict, encourage trust and transparency, and create a safe space for courageous conversations—all of which cultivate a better sense of belonging.

Restorative circles, used by courts, prisons, schools, and others, are based on the belief that what we need to enhance or even repair relationships will evolve naturally through dialogue in a circle. The "Circle Keeper" formulates questions for the circle. A "talking piece" is passed to give everyone a chance to speak. No one interrupts. No one is required to speak, but everyone is invited to do so. All participants are treated equally, regardless of rank or title. By building a foundation of wisdom based on shared stories, experiences, and perspectives, the circle becomes a container—strong enough to *hold* emotions that are difficult to process.

In circles, there are "shifts," moments of enlightenment. Sometimes, we "shift" because of what we share. The most meaningful way we connect with others is to share our stories. Sometimes, our ability to "hold space" for someone else's story is what we need to discover something about ourselves. Circles not only reveal our own suffering but also how we have harmed others. Sometimes anger enters the circle, which is necessary to express. Anger can be a catalyst to release toxins, move beyond pain, and even open our hearts to forgiveness.

Judge Raymond E. Kramer and his colleagues Sethu Nair, Halley Anolik, and Justo Sanchez were the first people to introduce the power of restorative circles to me. They are part of the [Center for Creative Conflict Resolution at OATH](), which provides NYC agencies with positive, inclusive ways to resolve conflict. The Citywide Roundtable Leadership Council is a vital resource for the leadership of restorative circles. Other significant resources include the [Restorative Justice Initiative](), [Hidden Water](), and the [Visioning B.E.A.R. Circle Intertribal Coalition]() led by Strong Oak Lefebvre and others. "Grandmother Strong Oak" uses "Walking in Balance with All Our Relations" to help train others to use restorative circles. Restorative circles help heal the trauma of racism and the systematic marginalization of indigenous people. New York City recognizes the importance of restorative practices by requiring all city agencies to use them. Like Detroit and Oakland, several other cities are considered "restorative cities" because they utilize restorative practices in a number of their services, systems, and programs.

The first time I used restorative circles was to address conflict. I later realized that circles are equally important to build community and heal harm. By passing the talking piece, we can listen to concerns that we would not otherwise hear. We can offer resources to those we would not otherwise know are in need. We can renew ourselves and regain awareness of our purpose simply through the process of sharing with others. Most importantly, passing the talking piece in circles and honoring whatever needs to be processed builds a strong community of solidarity for whatever needs to be addressed. Circles interwoven in culture are always available to address conflict and heal harm.

Healing circles are based on the indigenous teachings and values of the Tlingit and Tagish people of Canada, who taught author and teacher Kay Pranis and authorized her to teach the peacemaking circle process. I was trained in circle-keeping by [Elizabeth Clemants](). [Her restorative circle intensive]() was one of the most powerful experiences I have ever had. Not only did I learn technique, but I also experienced the benefits of the circle as a participant. I developed more clarity regarding my relationships with others, deeper insight on how to move forward with my goals, and most importantly, the weight of several emotional burdens that I carried were lifted. Clemants, who also works with Michelle Gutierrez, does phenomenal work. I was also trained by Grandmother Strong Oak and her team, who provided a powerful training of indigenous practices that address both racial injustice and sexual violence and help heal body, mind, soul, and Spirit with restorative circle practices.

Courageous conversations about race and other demographics in the safety of a circle are important because we live and work in a multi-cultural society and thus must engage in meaningful racial dialogues with one another. Dr. Derald Wing Sue, the author of *Race Talk and the Conspiracy of Silence*, says encountering "diverse racial points of view, being able to engage in racial conversations, and successfully acknowledging and integrating different perspectives leads to an expansion of critical consciousness."

Sharing our individual stories engage the cross-racial interactions and dialogue necessary to increase racial literacy and dispel misinformation. Some of the best healers will emerge during circles, like my friends and colleagues, Atoia, Yomi, Kobie, Giselle, Brooke, Telina, Steven, and Tray: who are prophets of wisdom that must be shared and truth that must be spoken. We must build a strong container to hold space for healing our lives and the deep-seated racism tearing our country apart.

Circle Rules

I was trained in holding circles in person, but since the pandemic, I have been in some of the most powerful, transformational circles that have been virtual. Here are some of the essential rules for circles. Everyone is equal. No person is more important than anyone else. There is a Circle Keeper, but the keeper participates in the circle and merely guides the process.

Emotional aspects of individual experiences are welcome.

For virtual circles, the order of participation is put in the group chat, but the chat is not used by participants except to note the entries by the circle keepers (*e.g.*, the circle order or the prompt/question) or administrative emergencies (someone is not audible or has to depart early). All participants should be visible via video camera unless they are having technical difficulties and participants are comfortable that they are who they say they are.

The "keeper" leads the circle by making introductory comments and poses the questions ("prompts") to guide the discussion. As mentioned, the keepers are full participants. Generally, one or two keepers can be used. More keepers can be designated to hold space for healing in potentially difficult circles. A talking piece is introduced by the keeper and passed with a hand motion. Keepers should select talking pieces in advance, which are usually objects with significance to the speaker (*e.g.*, sweetgrass, crystal, a Native Talking Stick, a medal, a stone, a child's toy, a book, etc.).

The only person authorized to speak is the person holding the talking piece (one person at a time). Participants may pass and choose not to speak during a round and share in a subsequent round of questions. When a person is finished speaking, they pass the talking piece to the next person. Cross-talk, speaking out of turn, or even putting something in the chat to comment on what someone shared is prohibited. Passing the talking piece around the circle should allow everyone a chance to share what comes up for them in response to the prompt and/or what others have shared. The circle rules have helped preserve the sanctity of the circle for years, supporting deep listening and reflection.

The beginning or "Circle Openings" set a positive tone for participants to transition into the circle process. Examples of Circle Openings include the recitation of poems, quotes, or stories, or mindfulness techniques. During openings, circle keepers share Circle Rules if participants are unfamiliar with them. The basic rules include the following: "Respect the talking piece" (everyone listens, everyone has a turn to speak); "Speak from the heart" (your truth, your perspectives, your experiences); "Listen deeply" (be patient, your truth is also revealed through other shares); "Trust that you will know what to say"(no need to rehearse mentally); and "Don't ramble" (be concise and considerate of the time of others).

Conversations about racism are powerful subjects for circles because all participants can share without judgment by other circle members, who must listen without interruption and are not supposed to attack or argue with the person holding the piece.

Speaking from one's own experience is paramount. My experience with circles supporting racial inclusion has been powerful. The safe spaces that circles provide are an important step towards building a more inclusive work environment.

Some suggested prompts for circles on racial inclusion are as follows: Did you know that race is a construct? What would you like to share about racial inclusion? How can you help improve racial inclusion and equity? Have you ever suffered from imposter syndrome? What is your learning edge in becoming more inclusive? How will you care for yourself between this circle and the next? What would you like to see done to combat racism in the world? How can you be a better ally for BIPOC colleagues? How can your organization help improve racial inclusion in one year? For any question, you can follow with an additional round by asking, "Did anything else come up for you?" if you feel participants need to share more.

To close, there can be a one-word "check-out" that brings closure for each participant. A "Closing" can also be provided as closing remarks. Circle keepers should ensure that everyone takes responsibility for making the circle a welcome, safe place for open dialogue. Keepers can emphasize that "we all have something to learn from each other." Each circle should have a definition of crosstalk as part of the guidelines. Participants can reference a share by saying, "when you brought up X, it brought up Y for me." Otherwise, there should be no comparisons, and caution should be exercised to refrain from being judgmental. Wisdom from the circle can be shared but not the specifics of what someone said. No one should discuss shares outside of the circle.

The goal is not to garner validations but to foster a space of integrity and vulnerability. When we are vulnerable, we encourage an even exchange. The focus in circles remains on ourselves, using first-person statements like *I think*, *I feel*, and *I need* to share our own experience, strength, and hope.

*Take a moment and envision a circle
for deep listening.*

*What questions would you want to ask
if someone else's answer would reveal to you
something about yourself?*

*What would you need to make sure
that a circle space is safe for you?*

*What theme would you cover in circle
to help make the world more inclusive?*

THE POWER OF INCLUSION

• CHAPTER 6 •

Share

*Inclusion welcomes everyone's story
but is also creative enough
to tell a new one
and generous enough
to embrace the edges of others
with shared strength.*

Circles are one of the most powerful vehicles to tell our stories because they create safe spaces where everything is supposed to remain in confidence, without judgment. Native Americans teach when we learn each other's stories, our stories change. Our stories teach us to believe in ourselves and uncover the wisdom from all our relations, including animals, plants, and the entire universe. When we share our stories, we not only tear down the walls between us but create a healing balm of truth.

We are all storytellers. Storytellers are healers. Stories offer the sanctuary of re-opening wounds and healing them; sharing joy and being lifted in it; finding logic in what appeared illogical, and learning from it.

When I was a girl, we did not have a lot of material things, but my siblings and I had stories that we shared. Even though we did not know our Native American Grandmothers, Strong Oak, Nancy, Margaret, and many others, storytelling was in our DNA. The power of the word, the *nommo*, is in both our Native American and our African roots. Enslaved Africans had to rely on memory, witness, and testimonials because they were prohibited from reading. Our culture is an oral tradition of work songs, field songs, spirituals, gospel, blues, jive-talking, jazz, hip hop, rap, and spoken word in all shapes and forms. As I listen to the stories Grandmother Nancy shares, I feel their miracles, carrying words that need to be heard and good medicine that heals our souls.

As a teenager, I was taught to share my story by the late Frances Hamburger, my speech coach at Cass Technical High School in Detroit. I learned the value and the humility of sharing from the heart and realized my own story was more meaningful than big words or intellectual quotes. She taught me how to uplift the truth as inspiration to others and how to weave that truth with the beauty of poetry, cultural pride, and the aspiration of the American dream. Through her constant guidance, I learned that our stories motivate, inspire, and teach but, most importantly, heal.

When I share my story, I offer vulnerability, which creates a safe space for others to share. When someone else shares, I embrace their story, and because of the trust we build, my story is no longer my own. I leave it with them, and if something in me needs to be healed, I am closer to healing because releasing my pain in a safe space offered me an opportunity to begin again.

We must be courageous enough to let our stories go and not be afraid to reveal who we are through our stories. In telling our stories, our job is to give to the audience, not take from them. The late Joseph Taormina, my public speaking and oral interpretation teacher, taught me the importance of confidence, embracing the audience, and grabbing their attention through compassion and empathy. In his classes and as part of the Cass Tech Readers' Theatre, I heard the best oral interpretations ever and experienced the most ingenious performances by other high school students. Even at a graduate level, I did not experience better storytellers than Cass Tech's Readers' Theatre.

Readers' Theatre provided the foundation for the way I tell a story, as well as how I listen to one. Know your material well enough so that you can connect with it through the heart. I believe that we must listen to ourselves enough times to connect our souls with what we share. The more we hear ourselves tell the story in our own private rehearsal, the better we will resonate with its truth and meaning, as well as its delivery to our audience. The nuances of delivery reveal themselves: when to pause, slow down, question, laugh, look deep into the audience, change voice, rhythm, pace, cadence, sigh, or paint a picture of words for all our senses.

But a story is more than a rehearsed presentation. A story is a tool of transformation that may paint a picture, teach a lesson, save a soul, or even ease a burden. In a circle, we deliver stories in a unique way, often revealing things we have never said before. We discover truths that surprise us because they have never been told, and we hold healing space for souls who must share their truth but cannot bear the telling alone.

CECILIA B. LOVING

*One of the most important aspects of sharing a story
is creating a safe space in which to tell it.
If we do not trust our audience,
we will hold back the most important details.*

"We speak to be heard and listen to know."

*If we pause a moment, before we share,
speak with honesty and compassion,
and make a commitment to hold space
for whatever comes up for us,
we allow the truth shared
to fill the spaces in our hearts,
and be held without judgment.*

What truth do you need to tell?

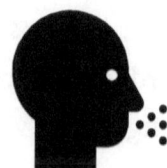

THE POWER OF INCLUSION

Allow Your Audience to Feel Your Experience

When we share our stories, it is important to focus on the five senses. What did you hear? What did you say? What did you see, what colors, shapes, textures did you experience? What did you taste, what foods, drinks, flavors? What did you smell? What did you touch? What sensations did you feel? When you remember your story in your body and tell it without notes or self-consciousness, your audience "relives" the story with you in heart and mind, which provides a connection. Storytelling is healing, so the best techniques for sharing stories are worth learning. Storyhood and Narativ provide some powerful storytelling tools.

One of the most important things in sharing your story is making sure that you convey it in the most empathetic manner so that it is genuine. One of my favorite ways to tell a story is through a poem, especially for those things too difficult to say directly. Poetry allows me to tell my story indirectly, with heart and meaning that cannot be expressed in prose. I also like to document my stories through articles, so I believe that the most important initiatives for DEAI are the stories we share through newsletters, Ted Talks, books, infographics, testimonials, blogs, speeches, plays, and video messages, screensavers, reports, and courses.

While doing an exercise led by the NYC Office of Creative Conflict Resolution, I was asked to select a partner in a group I thought was most different from me and exchange stories about our likes and dislikes. I chose a White male officer in Fire Prevention as my partner, and to my surprise, we had an incredible amount in common. It was a great lesson in how storytelling helps remove the barriers of perceived differences. We both enjoyed nearly all of the same things. Our stories are gifts that reveal the common ground we share, the most vulnerable teaching moments, and the values that inform our wisdom. We never know who someone is until we hear their story.

*What three struggles in your life
are you willing to share?
What are three things that you love the most, hate the most,
fear the most, make you laugh the most, or desire the most?
What is the medium in which you prefer to tell your story?*

• CHAPTER 7 •

Forgive

*Inclusion releases its tethers from the past,
those ties that bind bitterness,
and trap it where its power sits
waiting for us to take control
of our own fate,
realizing that by the act of forgiving others,
we liberate ourselves.*

One of the most important lessons from our stories is forgiveness. Forgiveness is not for the person we need to forgive. Forgiveness is for us. When we hold resentment against anyone, we bind ourselves to that person. By being resentful, we give that person or situation our energy. We give them so much power over us that we drain the energy we would use on the tasks we need to accomplish. To redirect our energy, we have to see the person or situation in a new way, without ill feelings, regret, or resentment. When we act with forgiveness rather than condemnation, we are not distracted but are energized by a clean slate.

As Bishop Desmond Tutu sets forth in *The Book of Forgiving*, forgiveness is not a weakness; it is a strength. It requires courage and strength to release people and situations who have harmed us. People will always live with the consequences of their actions. Processing forgiveness is not quick; it does not require us to forget, deny, nor pretend that something did not happen. Forgiveness does not deny history nor refrain from seeking justice.

People are in our lives for a season, a reason, or a lifetime and when that period ends, we must let them go. We cannot control the way people make decisions, and we must respect them for who they are, regardless of our differences. Sometimes people will not accept us for who we are; however, that is not a sign we need to change. We cannot change other people; they do that for themselves. But we can change how we allow others to impact our lives.

In his book *Happiness: A Guide to Developing Life's Most Important Skill*, Ricard Matthieu, one of the world's most learned experts on happiness, says that "while it may be difficult to change the world, it is always possible to change the way we look at it." Hatred for others harms us even more than them and adversely impacts our happiness because we are created for the connection of fellowship.

Whatever the challenge, we need to let go of the past. By releasing the toxins of resentment, we free ourselves to move forward: physically, emotionally, and spiritually. Forgiveness not only releases the energy that is blocked by our anger but becomes an important part of our spiritual development. The more we practice it, the easier it gets.

We need to learn from the past and address injustice, but that doesn't require us to ruminate in anger or despair. When we assault another's humanity, we assault our own humanity. Bishop Tutu says, "[e]very person wants to be acknowledged and affirmed for who and what they are, a human being of infinite worth, someone with a place in the world. We can't violate another's dignity without violating our own. Violence, whether in words or deeds, only begets more violence. Violence can never engender peace." Restorative practices heal both harmer and harmed. In the same manner, we must forgive others, we need to be forgiven. We have all been harmed, and we have all harmed others.

Research shows that ruminating about grudges is just as stressful as the actual experience. The physical benefits of forgiveness seem to increase with age. According to a study by Loren Toussaint, people over 45 years of age who had forgiven others reported greater satisfaction with their lives and were less likely to report feelings of nervousness, restlessness, and sadness.

Forgiveness does not involve excusing another person's actions or forgetting what happened. To forgive is not the same as to reconcile. Reconciliation is a negotiation strategy in which two or more people come together again in mutual trust. You may choose not to reconcile with the person you are forgiving. Forgiveness is letting go of your emotional ties to the past so that you can move forward, unencumbered, into the future. Telling our stories is part of the way that we process forgiveness. Whether we forgive and how we forgive is a process that unfolds at the heart of the stories we tell and the insight we gain from them. Choose the story that you will tell.

CECILIA B. LOVING

*Take a moment and breathe into the now.
Your time focusing on the breath is a sanctuary.
Count to four on the inhalation,
and to six on the exhalation.
repeat this several times.
Think of a person who harmed you.
Breathe in whatever caused you pain,
and then release it in the breath.
See the fear, frustration, and disappointment
that they caused you,
and breathe it away
in a simple breath.
Repeat this several times,
and then, allow the healing light of
love to fill you
mind, body, and soul.*

• CHAPTER 8 •

Thank

*Gratitude is not merely a thank you
but energy that attracts more to be grateful for,
knowing thanks is not hollow
but is the heart of giving.*

Gratitude is important to inclusion; it opens our hearts and melts our defenses. Whatever we give thanks for multiplies and gives way to the greater good. If we are alive and breathing, we have something to praise and give thanks for. Gratefully, we have a holiday that reminds us to be thankful. But we still forget the importance of gratitude. Giving thanks is powerful for the person that we thank but also for ourselves. Through gratitude, we center in the love of giving and, through that energy, align with the synergy of absolute good.

Giving thanks aligns us with the flow of calm, peace, and thus less stress and better health. Science supports that the more grateful we are, the better our physical health. Our hearts work better when we are more grateful. We sleep better. We are not as tired. We are less swollen. We even heal quicker. Our emotional well-being improves.

Gratitude reduces toxic emotions, like jealousy, resentment, frustration, regret, loneliness, and even depression. Being grateful makes us healthier and happier. Robert Emmons, a leading expert on gratitude, says that a daily practice of gratitude, like keeping a gratitude journal, bolsters our immune system, reduces aches and pains, lowers our blood pressure, increases our exercise regime, results in higher levels of positive emotions, makes us more alert, alive, and awake, gives us more joy and pleasure, results in more optimism and happiness, helps us be more generous, compassionate, and forgiving.

I am not a scientist but just based on a quick Google search, the science supports that we live longer when we are grateful. At a minimum, we live better. We are more empathetic. We have greater emotional intelligence. We suffer less from depression, substance abuse, and even PTSD. We are more resilient. Our health and well-being are improved.

We cannot tell our loved ones, colleagues, and others "thank you" too much. We can practice gratitude verbally or in writing, such as by writing letters of gratitude each week. We can keep a gratitude journal, which only requires us to jot down a few grateful sentiments before sleep. We can thank our family and friends for the little things: the terrific lunch they shared; the great job they performed; the joy they brought; the story they shared; the changes they initiated, no matter how small.

Gratitude is not merely saying thanks. Gratitude is a catalyst of transformation, providing a lens of a greater appreciation of everyone and everything within our experience. Our history, experiences, family, education, environments, media, and so many other elements fill us with the toxins of shame, blame, and bias. Just as much as we are biased against others, we are also biased against ourselves. Giving thanks is another way to heal, restore, and rejuvenate.

Gratitude is not merely an emotion; it is causative energy. We should give thanks because someone has done something for us and because by thanking them, we connect with the good of unlimited source that is everywhere present, which attracts *even more* good. We should give thanks because the universe keeps giving to us in remarkable ways and because when we give thanks, we open up a well-spring of energy that pours even more blessings our way. We should give thanks because it is the right thing to do in exchange for our many blessings and because gratitude opens our hearts to receive good. A grateful mind is not only a *great* mind that attracts to it *great* things, but it is a mind that has the highest point of view, the truth that abundance is everywhere present.

Giving thanks is the spigot that we turn on, the switch that we tune into, the supply that we tap, the channel that we open to receive the infinite supply and absolute good we desire.

Take a moment and pause in gratitude for everything, everyone, and every situation that has brought you to this moment. In this breath of appreciation, stop worrying and regretting and instead connect a higher purpose whose goal is to fill you with joy and happiness.
Send gratitude to everyone who comes to your mind, especially those difficult to thank.
Send an email, text, or note to someone of another background, culture, or religion, preferably someone to whom you have never given thanks.

• CHAPTER 9 •

Balance

*Inclusion walks in balance
to honor the sacredness
of being part of all our relations,
recognizing each aspect
of who we are,
blessing the entire planet.*

W alking in balance is a way to relate to everything and everyone. We are not separate from the earth, from plants or animals, nor separate from each other. Everything and everyone is "related" to us. The illusion of being separate makes us feel disconnected from our power of being one with "all our relations" and the reciprocity of connecting to each one, in Spirit, body, and mind.

If we depend on intellect alone, we limit ourselves to the ego and fail to grasp the wisdom of the Spirit and body. Limited to the ego, everything we give is clouded by the artificiality of judgment, self-centeredness, and selfishness. We focus on competition rather than community. If we depend on the physical alone, we are limited to what we see in the flesh, what spiritual teachers call "the appearances of things," and ignore what we are informed by mind and Spirit. If we follow Spirit but not the body, we ignore the ecology of maintaining ourselves physically and the earth mother on which we dwell. Balance requires the reciprocity of being in synch with all the dimensions that make up who we are: spiritual beings having a human experience, the collective wisdom of unlimited gifts and talents, and reverence for the earth temple and the temple of our bodies that house the spirit of the land and the souls of humanity.

If some aspect of our well-being falls out of order, it is an opportunity to heal ourselves by balancing all our dimensions. The same balance is required of the four directions, the elements and seasons, and how they impact our health. The physical ties to our indigenous roots appear severed by hatred, greed, racism, murder, and terrorism. But nothing can destroy the spirit of our ancestry's tie to us. Physical trauma cannot dissolve the deep spiritual roots of who we are, where we came from, and how the grandparents we may not have known continue to guide us through whatever we experience, including racism, slavery, reservations, camps, and caste systems. We stand on their vision, hope, love, and strength. When we open ourselves to an awareness of who we are, we tap the power of our ancestors to heal what still needs healing, fix what needs fixing and accept the unlimited power of the universe as our own. When we honor our ancestors, we are guided to walk in balance.

Walking in balance requires us to be visionary, to leave norms, conventions, and rigidity to create a world that honors everyone and everything. We have access to the strength of all our relations throughout the world, all cultures, languages, expressions, and traditions, and all that they teach us. When we are not inclusive, we fail to experience all aspects of who we are, and we do not give to the parts of us most in need. On a personal level, balance calls us to honor the entirety of who we are and our connection to the entire planet. Balance invites us to care for our whole self by receiving from and giving to all our relations.

Illness largely begins in our minds, which we can change. In the scripture, Jesus says that it is not what we put in our bodies that defiles us but what comes out. In other words, as *Walk in Balance: The Path to Healthy, Happy, Harmonious Living* by Sun Bear, Crysalis Mulligan, Peter Nufer, and Wabun teaches us, it is not what we eat but what eats us that makes a difference.

Anger, guilt, shame, blame, turmoil, sadness, and frustration have their place on our path from harm to healing, but we cannot live on them. Balance gives us a way to release the toxic energy of whatever does not serve us mentally, physically, or spiritually. We have to release the fear, worry, doubt, violence, animosity, hatred, shame, blame, and guilt and live in the power of all our relations. We do not have the strength to do what needs to be done alone. Without balance, we live in the toxic energy of too much or not enough, the messiness of lower vibrations. The healing energy of balance is one of the powers of inclusion because it makes us pay attention to our entire being in the same manner that we need to embrace the entire planet.

When we welcome, uplift, and support ourselves—spirit, body, and mind, we accomplish the first step in welcoming, uplifting, and supporting others. Healing, transformative energy begins with us. The power of inclusion includes recognizing our greatness, which is paramount to seeing the greatness of others.

I have scattered the seeds of prayer here, as Spirit leads me, to uplift the power, presence, and purpose of all our relations. I did not know my grandparents, but here I hear the cadence of Grandmother Strong Oak's prayers, who leads Walking in Balance, and the power of how she blesses each one of us to do the work of racial justice and healing. I am grateful for that part of me that is indigenous to this land. At this time, like no other, we need to feel the power of all our relations.

Oh Grandmothers and Grandfathers of the North,
we thank you for your winters,
the falling silence of wisdom that covers us in a new awareness,
the balance of nature's abundance
that teaches us we have enough.

Oh Grandmothers and Grandfathers of the East,
we are lifted in the grace of your awakening,
your springtime of rebirth and recreation.

THE POWER OF INCLUSION

We are grateful for the fire that the season gives us
its new growth, its rain,
its blossoms of encouragement,
and all of the plants
and animals,
fed, encouraged
and revived by spring's resurrection
of renewal.

Oh Grandmothers and Grandfathers of the South,
we thank you for your warmth of love,
how it summons us to our sense of community,
compassion and preparation of days ahead,
how it allows us to see ourselves in all people
regardless of how they see themselves.

Oh Grandmothers and Grandfathers of the West,
we reap the autumn of new fruit,
and paint ourselves red in the leaves of your harvest,
finding new abilities and cultivating them –
while realizing the need to release
what no longer serves us.

CECILIA B. LOVING

Balancing the Spirit

When we recognize our power as spiritual beings, we realize our oneness with all humanity. Recognizing the power that we are as human beings does not start with what we experience in the flesh but with the recognition that we are spiritual beings having a human experience.

Our relations have shared teachings throughout time that the balance we need in our lives begins with Spirit. Do you understand the power that you are? Respecting the truth that you are a spiritual being having an experience in a physical world will not answer all your questions immediately, but it is a starting place. Spirit as our counselor, teacher, and guide shows us the path to heart and meaning. Spirit, or whatever you call higher consciousness, Divine Mind, Absolute Good, God, Jehovah, Allah, I AM, Krishna, Ra, Buddha, provides a fulcrum for achieving balance.

Scientists have discovered that we are all energy with the power to change our experiences, bodies, and existence. In Luke 4:23, Jesus is quoted as saying, "physician heal thyself." When we do not include Spirit, in whatever manner spiritual energy reveals itself to us, as part of our daily routine, we are overtaken by the toxic energy of what we see happening around us, with a sense of weakness and exhaustion that we do not have the power to bring about change. I see and hear so many colleagues and friends saying that they are exhausted, tired, nearly depleted from the racial justice and inclusion work that must be done to experience greater harmony, peace, and compassion for everyone.

As our ancestor civil rights activist Fannie Lou Hamer said, "I am sick and tired of being sick and tired." She was a living testimony to the power of Spirit as no matter what confronted her, she said, "I'm not backing off." Spirit re-energizes us. We are constantly revitalized by the unlimited power of Spirit, which many refer to as "Absolute Good."

All civil rights movement leaders were anointed with the unlimited power of Spirit to accomplish their work. There is no question that Rev. Dr. Martin Luther King, Jr. was a man of Spirit. Harriet Tubman was a woman of Spirit. Nelson Mandela was a man of Spirit. Gandhi was a man of Spirit. Malcolm was a man of Spirit. The work of inclusion, racial equity, and justice, welcoming and uniting everyone, is not merely a physical battle; it is spiritual work. Spirit is essential to our balance and ability to cross the finish line of success.

Dr. King said I have seen the promised land. Recognizing the power of Spirit does not divide us according to how we choose to experience Spirit from our religious culture or creed but is the essential first step that we must make, guided by the truth that awakens us. King was a Christian; Gandhi was Hindu; Malcolm was Muslim; Jesus was a Jew, but all shared the inexhaustible Spirit that gave them the enlightenment, fortitude, and miracles that they needed.

Many of us begin our day with a devotional, prayer, or meditation. We must honor our Muslim family, who prays and re-centers throughout the day, which is a lesson in discipline for us all. This practice centers us in the greatness of Spirit expressing as us. Our Master Teachers reveal Spirit can do no more for us than it can do through us. We must center ourselves daily so that we are receptive to a higher presence. All healing begins with Spirit, which teaches us that we are already whole. We are already one, not only one person who is one with Spirit (meaning nothing separates our connection with whatever we perceive as God, Spirit, or whatever you call the Divine), but we are also one people united beyond the differences of our appearances.

For some of us, our oneness with Spirit is difficult to fathom because we have been taught that we are not worthy. Balancing Spirit as an essential part of who we are welcomes us to our worthiness. We will not feel welcome to the table of inclusion unless we believe our contribution is just as important as the contribution of other guests. When we know that "we are gods," we show up as our powerful best selves, filled with the light, presence, and truth of our greatness.

We cannot come to the dance and move like Bill T. Jones, or Katherine Dunham, or Josephine Baker, or Alvin Ailey, or the best dancers, movers, and shakers of our various cultures unless we are one with the unlimited power of our Spirit. The power of inclusion is not merely about being invited, but when we show up daily as our best selves for ourselves as one with Spirit, we embody the truth that the dance requires no invitation because the dance is wherever we are.

Spirit does not allow us to dwell in weakness or inadequacy. Spirit is not tired, deflated, or defeated because it is the greatest power that there is. Have you taken a moment today to recognize your greatness, which is the unlimited power of Spirit expressing as you?

When we center in the breath that connects us all, we can slow down and be aware of our sisters and brothers without judgment. We can approach the altar of forgiveness with unconditional compassion and spare no one the power of love emanating from our hearts, by our touch, in our eyes, as our voice. We start by loving haters seventy-seven times and more. We can raise ourselves from the delusion of our own fears and touch 'the hem' that finds in us the true meaning of peace.

What would we ask of the love that is our own being, whose blessings line every cell, molecule, atom, and ether of who we are? When we are balanced, we know that we have all that we need, and no one and nothing can deprive us of it. The manner that we connect with Spirit is just as inexhaustible as its supply. Choose what works best for you.

The following is what works best for bringing the balance of Spirit into my life:

I center in the breath of prayer as part of meditation. Without this center of oneness, I am more vulnerable to the toxic energy around me. This is a practice that is best done as soon as I rise. In the Spirit, I acknowledge my wholeness.

I speak words of power through affirmations with purpose. We have the power to decree a thing and make it so. Some call it praying boldly or speaking truth to power. Speaking truth to power reconnects us with the greatness of who we are.

I memorialize the affirmations in my journal, which may take the shape of a blog, book, story, poem, circle, or other ideas.

I move through prayers as my walk, weightlifting, yoga, stretch, dance, qi gong, tai chi, elliptical machine, or whatever else I need to move through to realize the presence and power of God energizing me. Prayer is a practice that we can use daily. Prayer wakes us up, bathes, dresses, cleans, works, ends, and begins in, as, and through us. We can pray without ceasing.

These practices fortify our connection to the truth that we are one. In the practice of the love of Spirit, we move beyond the confines of just thinking about ourselves and enlarge our capacity to bless others. When we are one with Spirit, we appreciate each other and send each other the energy of perfect health and wholeness simply by our own daily practice. In realizing that we are all part of one Spirit that blesses us, we are healthier, stronger, and more resilient.

We can be as creative as we like in our prayers, affirmations, meditations, and movement. The prayer shell on the adjacent page is one that I learned as a teen at the Home of Love in Detroit, led by the spiritual activist and radio disc jockey, Martha Jean the Queen. The framework is what I used to guide my prayers as a teen, a framework that I still use now on occasion.

As mentioned above, the sacred text says, "I am in the Father, and you are in me, and I am in you" (John 14:20). For me, prayer is an acknowledgment of our oneness. My theology encourages oneness rather than fear. I am intentional in repeating this scripture, not only because it is a favorite but because it is the truth. We are all one with Spirit. The power of inclusion recognizes the oneness that we share. When our words and thoughts guide us to realize that we are one, we balance body and mind with the power of knowing no one and nothing can stop us from doing the good that we are here to do.

*Dear Mother, Father, Everything, Almighty God,
Oh, how I love you, and how I praise your Holy Name.
Please forgive me for each and every unkind thought, word, or deed that I may have expressed knowingly or unknowingly against You, myself, or any one of Your children.
[INSERT THE DESIRES OF YOUR HEART.
E.g., I uplift a new community of faith, one that sees beyond fear to love, beyond exclusion to inclusion, beyond separation to the truth that we are one.
I acknowledge the light that we are summoned to shine, like the city on the hill, for all to see.]
I am grateful because I know
what I have prayed for is already done.
It is done, it is done, it is done, and so it is, so let it be.
Amen.*

Balancing the Body

Respecting others begins with respecting ourselves, starting with the person we see in the mirror. Respecting our physical bodies with compassion requires that we care for our bodies. We must be mindful of what we need to do to release the tension and toxins of the world and center in the temples of our being. Release is a vital part of balancing our physical needs with perfect health and wholeness. Unless we release doubt, worry, and despair, our bodies will carry that trauma.

Not only are we carrying our pain but also the trauma of our ancestors. This inner guilt, shame, and blame detract from our ability to honor our wholeness. The good news is that we can start anew, respecting our physical bodies in a new way, right at this moment, right where we are. We can release and let go of mistakes, doubts, and trepidation and be uplifted in courage, creativity, and compassion. We always have the power to release our past transgressions and put on a new self.

The power of inclusion makes us realize that it does not matter who we are or what we have experienced in the past: we are all given a choice to improve ourselves. We are already whole, and exercising the choice to express our wholeness is always available to us. We always have a blank slate to begin again, to honor who we are in the flesh with respect and reverence. When we do so, we bring that renewed vigor, perspective, and presence to everything we do.

When I was in the eighth grade, I remember making a conscientious decision to change, and I did. In a single moment, I reflected on my life and the type of person I wanted to be, and I changed. Several teachers commented on the new me with astonishment. I was surprised that they noticed. At age 12, it meant choosing not to give my energy to being accepted by the popular crowd but being determined instead to be independent, learn as much as possible, and do my best. The teachers witnessed something in me that shifted. They knew I had changed on the inside, as well as on the outside.

Our right to choose who we want to be is something we all can do. Some might call these instant changes "miracles," seeing them as unattainable. But miracles are love, waiting to use us as a vehicle through which to express. The ability to be our best and give our best to others is something we can all do. Our ability to choose, create, and be compassionate through communication makes us different from our oldest ancestors, the plants and animals who have dwelled on earth, much longer than us. We have the power to decide.

We are individual representations of a whole, an entire race of people filled with unique and individualized expressions. Yet, we are one. Our oneness connects us. Without that connection, it is difficult to survive. Many of us experienced that during the pandemic. We need to connect, even if only virtually. The connection we have with each other is also the emotional glue that heals and restores our bodies. We feel better when we realize that we are part of something greater than ourselves. We feel better when we give, speak, acknowledge, share, see, praise. We feel better when we are grateful. We feel better when we forgive. We feel better when we are inclusive. Inclusion is the epitome of our well-being.

Mother Earth reflects the oneness that we share and our potential as part of an ecosystem of a greater whole. Respecting one another is the starting point for releasing the trauma locked in our bodies. Only when we acknowledge the trauma of our ancestors, as harmed and harmer, can we release the pain that plagues the world. "How?" we ask. By honoring our bodies and the bodies of others, showing up as our best self by resting, rising, revitalizing, and remembering.

Rest

The pandemic called us to rest, take a time out from the "normal" rat race, and remember who we are: one people tasked with caring for each other. We shifted our priorities during the pandemic. We re-claimed our truth. We went to the edge of our tests, and we re-envisioned our purpose. But most importantly, we went within, and we rested from what we used to do to allow our new selves to emerge.

When we rest, we are more in tune with our collective wisdom. When we sleep, our dreams inform us; our subconscious mind guides us through symbols, emotions, and clarity. No matter what

I am having difficulty with the night before, I know just what to do when I awaken.

When I was 21 years old, a dream that I had guided me through every aspect of an upcoming challenge, so that when I experienced it, to my surprise, a few weeks later, I already knew the outcome. Within the last few years, one dream connected me with an ancestor who guided me and assured me that he was in a higher realm. The dream also gave me the important message of accountability to purpose: the need to do the work that we are here to do with integrity and honor. Upon awakening from dreams, I have been guided to do work and achieve results that I could have never achieved without rest.

We need rest from work. One of the most creative, productive, and ingenious people I worked with was a partner at a law firm who had a great ability to balance rest with work. As a young lawyer, I always thought he could rest because he was brilliant, but now I believe he was brilliant because he rested. Tom always made us take a break, even when we were in the middle of preparing for a trial. He would insist that we take the weekend off, and we would come back refreshed and rejuvenated for the work that lied ahead. He would not stay up all night working; he would rest. He would flawlessly examine witnesses and make arguments to the court with his rested mind, with little preparation.

Rest is trust. Rest is being in tune with the rhythm of a system greater than our individuality. The Psalmist says, "peace be still" because, in that stillness, we receive the truth. Rest allows the power of our greatness to re-energize our bodies and recharge our hearts and souls with a renewed vision to move forward. As theologians would say, even Jesus went away and rested for a while.

In rest, there is hope. In *Braiding Sweetgrass*, one of my favorite books, Native American poet, biologist, and storyteller Robin Wall Kimmerer tells the story of the pecan trees and how they feed us, not by being active each season but with rest. Only after rest do they flower and bless us with the bounty of their rich protein and fat and the hard storage shells that they come in, already protected to nourish us over time. With the bounty of the pecans after the trees have rested, there is food for everyone. The squirrels are fed and produce more baby squirrels. The hawks are fed by squirrels. Humans are fed by pecans and squirrels. But first, there was rest.

Even too much of a good thing can be bad. During the pandemic, we even had to rest from Zoom calls. I would rest my mind in a Netflix binge but then had to rest from technology. At 8:30 AM, I might find myself in a Zoom room of hundreds of people, so I never felt alone. But sometimes, I needed my camera off so that I could rest from being on display.

In a space where work and rest collide, establishing the proper boundaries to support the other can be difficult. When I worked in the living room, work seemed to take over my entire home, but I found rest in other parts of the house when I limited work to my home office. I could be away from work in the living room, dining room, or bedroom. Unconsciously, I never took work upstairs, where I rested from the day. These boundaries are important for how we live our lives beyond the pandemic. Rest from work is the only way we bring our best to it, so we must be careful about our tendency to take work home and drag it into those places we rely on for rest.

One of the best ways to rest from work is to play. Roger Mannix is a genius in combining play with emotional intelligence, giving us opportunities to bond and flow freely beyond our roles with creativity, movement, and freedom. Roger's company Ludolo teaches that play should be part of every curriculum for all ages. Play is not only related to the development of the brain's frontal cortex, which is responsible for cognition, but it also sparks our imagination.

Play fosters empathy and helps both children and the child in us develop new skills. One scientific study found that children who received an enriched, play-oriented parenting and early childhood program had significantly higher IQ at age five than a comparable group of children who were not in the program (105 vs. 85 points).

Seattle's Pike Place Fish Market is one example of a work environment that incorporates play in what they do. I have witnessed the fishmongers throw fish to one another in the open air, which is festive, fun, and engages the customers. It has a great impact on sales and strengthens relationships, attitudes, and mindset. There is even a leadership course based on the fish market called FISH.

When we rest from the seriousness of the task and enjoy what we do, we receive one of the best rewards: recognition and satisfaction from what we do. Rest is a key component of balance. Rest from rich foods gives us the ability to heal ourselves. Rest in water allows us to bathe in what we need and gives us nourishment by restoring our bodies. Returning to nature is a rest from the artificial conveniences of the indoors. Rest in circle allows us to connect with the truth that connects us all.

True balance allows us to take both short, medium, and long-term periods of rest. We can take a few minutes throughout the day to pause, restore, reflect, and laugh. We can also take an hour or two to retreat from work, like going to the gym, taking a walk through the neighborhood, sitting in the park, doing yoga, meeting a friend, or chatting on the phone. I am also a huge fan of retreats, even if they last for a day. I have gathered with colleagues at "Inclusion Innovation Labs" to laugh, center, enjoy and build more create the initiatives that we need through the "play" of brainstorming comradery, resting in the ease of revelation, insight, and freedom.

Rise

Rising is the energy of responsibility. In rising, we awaken to our truth, our calling, our vision, our purpose. We rise in the truth of what we must do, and we do it. When we rise, we take care of ourselves, of each other, and of the planet. I rise with more vision, energy, and enthusiasm after rest. I rise with more clarity, discernment, and connection with what must be done and exactly how to do it. With all the gifts that I receive after rest, I am astonished by my constant need to balance my ongoing desire to be productive with the need to rest.

Working at home is challenging for me because I rarely like to stop working. When I work at home, I miss the physical boundaries of moving between one location or another into a space dedicated to work, being in the physical presence of work colleagues. When I can move through community without restriction, I am also more disciplined about going to the gym, rising to the occasion to be my best physical self. Rising, however, is not merely moving; it is also about connecting with others. Rising is discerning what needs to be done and remaining steadfast to doing the requisite work to ensure its completion.

When we rise in the DEAI space, this means moving beyond mere compliance or Equal Employment Opportunity ("EEO") and doing the work that needs to be done regardless of the law and policy rules that guide our behavior. So many equate DEAI with EEO, which is essential but is merely a starting place.

EEO is a first step, a bare minimum—like a superficial reading of the Ten Commandments, basic rules of respect, honor, and decorum in how we treat each other. Thou shall not kill, for example, is a basic rule. Thou shall respect each other's relationships and property. But inclusion is how we live beyond the rules. In the ancient text, Jesus distinguishes between the law and "grace and truth" (John 1:17). Inclusion is how we show up to support one another beyond what is required: the grace and truth of being. When we rise to the occasion for others by being more inclusive, we also rise as our best selves.

Rising requires discipline, study, contemplation, and community engagement. Rest allows us to center in our greatness but rising is the call to tap it. When we rise, we are also more open and receptive to intuition, what I call divine guidance to offer creative solutions to problems.

Before I became aware of social scientists like Brené Brown's powerful work around shame and vulnerability, one of the most important intuitive thoughts I had was not to shame others around diversity and inclusion. We need to speak with honesty, truth, and conviction. We also need to express anger whenever that comes up for us, but we cannot languish in a state of anger. If we stay in a vibration of anger, we cannot focus on the work that must be done. When we sit in the emotion of anger, we stand in the way of our good, our best ideas, and our truth. Our truth does not lie in our anger but in the realization of our excellence. To repeat Einstein, "we cannot solve a problem at the level of the problem."

When we rise with balance within ourselves, we are collaborative, open, and willing to work to create a common ground for change and transformation. DEAI is not a priority for everyone. Unfortunately, it is generally seen through the lens of politics rather than the spiritual healing and connection it provides for each one of us. Until we confront the truth and heal the trauma of racism, we will remain in a state of shame. No one is better than anyone else, but the construct of White superiority created divides that cause people to believe in this untruth.

The time that healing takes is what inclusion is all about: building compassion, uplifting the importance of authenticity, providing safe spaces that guide us from harm to healing, moving being self-imposed silos (communities where we feel safe) to develop relationships with people beyond our "usual suspects," those stakeholders with whom we can find common ground to make a difference.

Rising is the energy that motivates us not only to talk but to listen, to not merely have answers but to be comfortable in simply asking the right questions with the vulnerability of not knowing. We have a lot to learn from those within our organization we rarely speak with, feel conflict from, or do not trust, and from people outside of our offices, organizations, and businesses who can help impact change. Rising gives us the incentive to create a culture of listening but moves beyond listening to be the synergy of healing.

Rising recognizes that we will make mistakes, but we can give ourselves permission to do our best to realize that the effort is worth the risk. The work of inclusion requires much more than the temporary band-aide of a leader, trainer, policy, program, committee, message, and/or group. We rise with a level of expectation that allows us to take our time and learn to love each other. These goals take commitment. Rising balances the sowing necessary to develop our ideas, achieve them, process their benefit, and repeat as often as possible to progress.

Rising is the impetus of solving problems beyond the mindset that created them. If we cannot solve the problem at the level of the problem, how can we solve it? We rise above our self-imposed limitations. We rise above fear. We rise above doubts. We rise above projecting our drama onto others and being at peace that we have what it takes to succeed.

Revitalize

We need to revitalize our bodies through self-care to be available to accomplish the work that needs to be done to honor the bodies of others. Our bodies tell us what we need to know, how to regenerate themselves, and how to heal. The problem is that we fail to listen, and even if we hear, we often fail to be obedient. Much of what we need to do is simple. Scientists say that our bodies continue to revitalize themselves and are always in a state of reinvention. Cells replenish. Old cells die. New cells form. Skin replaces itself. Our bodies are entirely new. Every cell is replaced. We aid the body's natural revitalization process with sleep, exercise, whole foods, sunshine, fresh air, water, and positive energy.

Revitalize with Sleep

To show up for anyone else, we must first show up for ourselves. We will not have the capacity to do our best, much less do right by anyone else, unless we are well and whole. Experts say that our brains cleanse the toxins during sleep, and we need 7-9 hours of sleep. To decrease the mind clutter and anxiety that comes with a stressful day, we are advised to turn off all electronic devices 30 minutes before bedtime.

Rather than watch something on an electronic device, we should read, journal, or meditate before sleep. Naps can compensate for lack of sleep, but naps should be at least 30 minutes to 1.5 hours to include deep sleep. Experts say that sufficient sleep helps eliminate dementia later in life. When we sleep, we are more in tune with what needs to be done to help with the wellbeing of everyone, and we build our capacity to get it done. When we include every aspect of our well-being as part of our regular routine, we build the foundation for being more inclusive.

THE POWER OF INCLUSION

Revitalize with Exercise

When we move, we re-charge our minds and cleanse the toxins from our bodies. Science shows that exercise increases the size of the hippocampus, which plays a role in emotional regulation. Exercising a minimum of three times a week for 30 minutes each time is sufficient to recharge your brain, increasing your ability to make complex decisions. So, movement benefits our brainpower.

Movement also helps reduce inflammation, which accelerates the aging process and what are considered "age-related" diseases. Temporary inflammation is the body's way of healing itself after an injury and protecting itself from infection. On the other hand, chronic inflammation is linked with all kinds of diseases, like diabetes, high blood pressure, or heart disease. When you start exercising and moving your muscles, your muscle cells release proteins that fight inflammation. It is also believed that the longer your workout, the more you decrease chronic inflammation.

Movement helps reduce your risk of heart diseases, lowers your blood pressure and triglyceride levels. Movement also helps manage blood sugar and insulin levels. Exercise can lower your blood sugar level and help your insulin work better. Movement strengthens your bones and muscles, slowing down the loss of bone density. Exercise is also known to reduce the risk of some cancers, including the colon. One of the great benefits I have also noticed is that exercise helps me sleep better, especially when lifting weights.

My goal is to exercise two hours a day, six days a week, in the gym. As I write this section, I have just returned from my neighborhood gym, having lifted weights, stretched, and done cardio. But I am back at the computer, which causes me to sit for long hours. I feel more balanced when I put in a few hours at the gym daily—weightlifting, stretching, and doing cardiovascular exercises, and when I have a second exercise period in the late afternoon or evening because I am sitting all day. But everyone should do what works for them.

Where we begin is determined by what our bodies need and what we enjoy doing. Sometimes I feel more balanced when I have a personal trainer to help me focus. Some may feel more balanced with a gym buddy. You can walk, hike, run, do yoga, play sports, lift weights, dance, skate, bike, jump on a trampoline, jump rope—whatever works for you. A great way to move and receive the nourishment of the sun and nature at the same time is to move through nature, which helps us maintain a peak physical, mental, and emotional state.

Revitalize with Nature

Vitamin D, known as the sunshine vitamin, is essential for optimal health and has many functions in the body. Spending a lot of time indoors and living in a colder climate can affect our ability to get Vitamin D from the sun alone. This vitamin plays multiple roles, such as assisting in promoting healthy bones and teeth, supporting immune, brain, and nervous system health, regulating insulin levels, and supporting diabetes management, to name a few.

It is always good to go outdoors and be with nature to find the balance that we need in our bodies. The ancient text reminds us of the beauty of lilies, simply being one without stress, strain, or toil.

Moving inspires, motivates, and increases our energy so that our bodies are revitalized, strengthened, and committed to the work that needs to be done. If you are not moving and can move, you need to exercise your muscles and strengthen them. If you need assistance moving, finding the best way to exercise and strengthen whatever you can move is imperative.

When we focus on the four directions of our indigenous traditions, we can experience the balance that is always teaching us through all our relations with the natural world. This includes the harmony of all plants and creatures. We listen and learn how to rest with balance through the four directions, move with balance, eat with balance, and drink with balance, in harmony with all creation.

Revitalize with Clean Eating

Nurturing the body through foods that bless us with honor for Mother Earth is vital to our health. This means eating the earth's energy through fresh fruits and vegetables and the protein and fat sources provided by the earth. This way of eating what is natural and organic to the land, rather than created by man, is a dietary plan based on foods eaten by hunter-gatherers. Many have studied the people who continue these ancient ways of hunting and gathering even today in regions of Africa, Asia, and other places that continue indigenous practices and have found that those who maintained the same practices as our indigenous ancestors do not suffer from most of the diseases that plague us today.

In Tanzania, for example, the Hadza are one of the remaining hunter-gatherer groups in the world who eat the same animals and plants that have been hunted and/or gathered for thousands of years. The nutrients our ancestors consume in regions like this are important because they shaped our immune system. Nothing is wasted or killed unnecessarily. The Hadza eat an amazing variety of plants, animals, and birds, which they can gather within a short amount of time. Nature does not provide a lot of carbohydrates that are man-made or sugar in the wild. Berries can be gathered, but they are low in sugar. Honey can be eaten, which grows in the wild but is not taken in excess.

By trial and error, I have found that a hunter-gatherer diet makes me healthier: a diet of berries, vegetables, fish, lean meats, especially grass-fed animals or wild game, and oils. I should avoid grains, such as wheat, oats, barley, legumes, beans, lentils, peanuts and peas, dairy products, refined sugar, salt, potatoes, and highly processed foods. The most important thing is to discover what works best for you. I respect the choices of others, which is what inclusion is all about.

When we are balanced, we do not over-compensate with one thing (*e.g.*, food, nicotine, caffeine, alcohol, narcotics, sleep, work, play) when we really need another. We are biologically required to be inclusive, balanced, and appreciate everything good for us instead of ignoring one thing at the sacrifice of something else. I like to work. I love my work in DEAI and how it demands that we think outside the box, step into the unknown, and be comfortable with being uncomfortable. But when I sacrifice rest for work, I suffer. When I stop sleeping to just do one more task, I am not at my best. The same is true for how we relate to others. Authenticity gives us balance. The beauty of being inclusive is that we receive the benefit of nutrients beyond the box of those we learned as part of our own traditions. We can all benefit from the wisdom of everyone.

THE POWER OF INCLUSION

Revitalize with Water

Dr. F. Batmanghelidj, author of *Your Body's Many Cries For Water: You're Not Sick; You're Thirsty* (www.watercure.com), treated more than 3,000 peptic ulcer patients with water alone and discovered that disease responds to water alone. Chronic dehydration is the root cause of most major degenerative diseases of the human body. Without the right amount of water to wash the acidic waste of metabolism, chaos results in our bodily functions, causing pain, Alzheimer's, stress, tumors, high blood pressure, high cholesterol, allergies, and other ailments. *These ailments can be healed with water.*

Even the scriptures indicate there is Spirit in water to sustain us, bless us, and heal us. Experts say that it is good to consume half the amount of your body weight in water ounces. If you weigh 100 pounds, you should consume 50 oz of water; if you are 200 pounds, you should be drinking 100 oz of water each day. If you work out, you must add at least a liter or 32 oz of water to every hour of exercise—on top of your daily requirement.

The literature says that the best time to consume water is 8 oz/a glass before consuming each meal and 8 oz/a glass an hour after each meal, and 8 oz/a glass water after eliminating water. A good gauge of whether we are getting enough water is the color of our urine: it is supposed to be colorless. If it is yellow—we are nearing dehydration; if it is orange – we are dehydrated. If it is brown, well, start drinking.

Revitalize with Positive Thinking

Positive thinking is viewing life as though everything exists to help us achieve our good. If our thoughts are negative, our outlook on life is more pessimistic. If our thoughts are mostly positive, we simultaneously receive many health benefits, such as longer life, less or no depression, better cardiovascular health, better resilience, and reduced stress. *How often do you focus on the negative instead of the positive? How often do you blame yourself? How often do you anticipate the worse?* All of these are ways that we sabotage positive thinking. We can think more positively by studying motivational teachings, watching inspirational movies, surrounding ourselves with positive people, listening to music, engaging in laughter, using affirmations, crying if we need to cry, smiling inside and outside, and getting to know those who are different.

Remember

Remembering who we are allows us to release the illusion that we are separate and know that we are one. If only Europeans remembered that those indigenous to this land are their people, their own brothers, and sisters who crossed the Atlantic hundreds of years before they did, then perhaps they would not have massacred their own relations. America had long been "discovered" by our indigenous grandmothers and grandfathers. If the "Pilgrims" remembered their own kin, would they have killed, slaughtered, and failed to learn the ancient teachings that would have helped this land experience its true greatness?

I have always been amazed by those who refer to indigenous people as savages and primitive. Our relationship with "all relations," especially those indigenous to the land and those who embody the truth, has vital wisdom to teach us. We need to remember that we are all from the same tribe called *homo sapiens*. Savage is how we treat others with animosity, violence, and hostility.

Scientists believe Neanderthals became extinct in northwestern Europe over 40,000 years ago due to competition, climate change, inbreeding, illnesses, and other failures to adapt—*perhaps including failures to cooperate*. Thus, every person on the planet can trace their roots to Africa, where humanity's great migration began over 60,000 years ago. Research shows that DNA, which originated from Africa, is the same DNA found in Europeans, Australians, Asians, Northern and Southern Americans, and everyone else.

The irony of this great migration is that scientists seldom credit the brilliance of our darker ancestors from Africa with the survival of humanity for thousands of years. We did not evolve from savages or apes, as some would like to believe, but with the "same advanced brains and nervous systems we have today, and with the ability to self-regulate vital functions already developed," explains Gregg Braden in *The Science of Self-Empowerment*. We just need to remember who we are because by so doing, we realize our great potential—to not merely populate this world but to expand throughout the entire universe.

Many scientists are learning from our African ancestors that cooperation and unity are the keys to the success of humanity. Our calling as caretakers of this planet is to live in peace, with compassion for each other, honoring our benevolence, ability to provide nutrition, safety, support, and education for each other. The disdain many of us have against the diversity of our languages, religions, sexual orientations, hair texture, cultures, skin colors, and the fictional belief that somehow one group or appearance is better than another is fear of the very connections that sustain us.

When we remember our grandmothers and grandfathers, whose genius, tenacity, innovation, and strength gave us the wherewithal to survive, we balance our own abilities with the oneness we share by our connection with each other. When I remember the power of our African grandmothers and grandfathers, I can release the trauma caused by those who came long after them and populated Australia, Asia, Europe, and all of the other lands of this planet, and be lifted in the vision, adventure, and wisdom of all our relations.

No one can explain how exactly our ancestors were able to migrate through harsh physical conditions and climates. Perhaps because they were not limited by the negativity and judgment that so often obscures our abilities and instead were informed by their higher spiritual consciousness of oneness ("at-one-ment") that continues to guide us when we are listening. We must remember that hatred and violence did not lead to our survival, nor will they enhance our continued success. Intuition, empathy, communication, and compassion, which require us to think with the heart rather than the ego, brought us across the waters and will carry us the rest of the way.

THE POWER OF INCLUSION

*Oh Grandmothers and Grandfathers of the North,
we feel your Spirit into our bodies from all directions,
grateful for the unity that you give us,
strengthened by the memory of our oneness.
We rest, rise, revitalize, and remember
the beginnings that gave birth to our species,
honoring the sanctity of our connection,
having forged the past for truth,
we call upon the "present,"
through the wisdom that is the future.
We honor our ancestors
whose spirits bless the planet in countless ways.*

*Oh Grandmothers and Grandfathers of the East,
we resonate in the body of all relations,
with the same breath
breathed through each one of us,
and the same vision through whose eyes we see,
guided by the view of the eagle,
the purpose from a higher vantage that excludes
nothing and no one.*

*Oh Grandmothers and Grandfathers of the South,
we ride the wind of your wisdom
as the perfection of creation,
as the whole being that we are,
revitalized with resilience.
We share the fight of the wolf:
fearless, tough, and cunning,
but also pure and loving and creative,
uplifted in water that cleanses the toxins
and opens all hearts with new faith.*

*Oh Grandmothers and Grandfathers of the West,
we remember the energy of the buffalo
and the great bison of our being,
the direction of sage, as safeguard, as prophet, as cleanser
of whatever is negative, as givers of good medicine.*

Balancing the Mind

We need sound minds to make decisions, but the egos that accompany our right to choose—throw our ecosystem out of balance. Our egos are our superficial consciousness, that part of us that we want the world to see. Our egos are amazing at trying to camouflage, make excuses, and stay comfortable in the appearances of things. Our egos are largely controlled by fear rather than love. Our egos can undermine "good sense," which many of us call "common sense." When I was growing up, my mother often made the distinction between people who operated with "book sense" (the ego) versus "common sense" (the heart). Only with the heart do we connect with everyone and everything in a holistic fashion. This sense of oneness is what provides balance to the mind.

"Oneness" is an appreciation for each other. We are not merely here to look good for ourselves but to be of service to everyone through what I call our "divine connection." When we realize our divine connection, we are more compassionate, vulnerable, and humble. We appreciate the good in everyone and thus exercise the best judgment to appreciate our differences and ability to help others instead of being guided by our egos.

Egos are part of our conscious minds, which help us make decisions. We also have an unconscious mind, which picks up the energies and vibrations around us. Our unconscious mind is more in tune with the unseen, the perceptions, intuitions, and epiphanies that we experience without physical evidence. One of the greatest things about getting older and wiser is that we are more confident. We trust our judgment. We are experienced enough to trust that we can rely on our abilities. We have a better understanding of what transpires around us.

Everyone is not blessed by the same amount of wisdom. So, everyone's ego is not guided or limited in the same way. Arguably, "old souls" are wiser. I remember when my ninth-grade history professor, Wendell Davis, dramatized this on the first day of history class. He used his hands to outline an imaginary door, and he explained that some people walk through this door into maturity, and some never will. Deep wisdom is the catalyst that takes us through the door and helps us control the fleshly, selfish desires of the ego, which is also tainted by biases of hatred and distrust of those different from us.

Our wisdom connects with the soul. The soul guides us with the pure consciousness of love, in which our bodies dwell. The soul speaks to the heart of our unconscious awareness and guides the ego to the extent it can. Sometimes it's difficult because the ego has a mind of its own. *The ego says, "I can't." The unconscious says, "I can." The soul says, "I am."* We live, move, and have our being in the soul.

Only with the soul's energy can we find the balance necessary to restore the harmony we need to heal our planet from bickering, fighting, and taking what is meant to be shared. We must restore the respect we once had for the land and collectively release the selfishness that thrives off putting the ego first. We balance our best when we learn to embrace the entire planet with our hearts.

As discussed earlier, the callings that emerge from our greater purpose are essential in discerning why we are here, having this experience in this time, space, and reality. Regardless of our gifts, they all evolve from our shared ability to give to each other. Balancing the mind requires that we restore our true potential and be resurrected or reborn as our best, authentic selves. Otherwise, we will subject ourselves to the inner critic of worthlessness and the despair of being less than. No matter who we are, we cannot allow the ignorance of others to minimize our self-worth, nor can we allow our egos to project invalidation on anyone else. It is important to remember that what we give, we receive. If we send negative, undermining thoughts to others, they are no more than a projection of what we believe about ourselves. Pride in our authenticity is not about the ego; it is about the soul.

With courage and fearlessness, we must quiet our egos. This alone will give us a confirmation of our roots and a validation of our worth. This sense of somebodyness means the refusal to be ashamed of being who we are. Our egos are not the doer of everything accomplished by us but the aspect of our consciousness connected with the material rather than the spiritual world. Only when we slow down and connect with the breath can we withdraw from the ego and unite with the spiritual. We are spiritual beings having a human experience. Connection with Spirit, our higher consciousness, is imperative.

By releasing the ego, which constantly thinks "me-me-me," we can focus on "us" and balance our obsession with what we desire with the greater good of what everyone needs and is here to contribute, what Gregg Braden calls "a greater, all-inclusive identity," in *The Wisdom Codes*. We have left the garden of wisdom and are entangled with the ego. The ego focuses on life through the lens of fear rather than love. In the ego, we cannot see the importance of the Beloved Community. Anything other than love is fear. Anything other than inclusion is exclusion.

When the ego is involved, we lose ourselves in the energy of fear and everything that accompanies it: resentment, jealousy, animosity, worry, anxiety, hatred, and all the other constructs devised by some to take from others. Race is a construct. Anything that makes us believe that we are better than other people is a construct. Balancing the need for egotistical accolades with the generosity of love, we see beyond the appearances of doubt and realize that this journey of inclusion is not about us but about the greater community that we are here to serve.

In the ancient text, Joseph is thrown into a pit and condemned to slavery by his own brothers. Yet, he becomes one of the most prosperous men in Egypt. Years later, his brothers seek Joseph's help, but they have no idea the person they beg is their brother. When the brothers recognize Joseph, they become afraid. But Joseph doesn't seek revenge. He does not operate by ego. Instead, in Genesis 50:20, Joseph tells his brothers, "don't worry, you meant it for evil, but God meant it for good." He feeds his brothers, balancing the ego with love, compassion, and forgiveness. Only by balancing the ego with the wisdom of love, compassion, and forgiveness do we cultivate the power of inclusion.

THE POWER OF INCLUSION

*Oh Grandmothers and Grandfathers of the North,
we release the burden of the ego
and instead are anointed by the power of your love,
knowing that race is a construct,
the ego is a construct,
fear is a construct,
and we always have available to us
the power to be united by compassion, humility, and kindness.
We rise from our slumber like the bear,
grateful to awaken to the truth of our oneness.*

*Oh Grandmothers and Grandfathers of the East,
we soar in this season of new beginnings,
filled with the grace of the fire
from which we were born.
We fly like great eagle
and we rise renewed by a new faith,
flying higher than our relations
could ever imagine.
We speak the truth of our power.*

CECILIA B. LOVING

*We balance Spirit, Body, and Mind,
with triumph, victory, and success.
We call on the power of all that is diverse,
equitable, accessible, and inclusive.*

*Oh Grandmothers and Grandfathers of the South,
we ride the wind of your wisdom
as the perfection of creation,
as the whole being that we are,
revitalized with resilience,
washed by the water
that cleanses the impure
and opens all hearts with new faith.*

*Oh Grandmothers and Grandfathers of the West,
we call the spirit of the great buffalo,
as safeguard, as prophet, as fortitude.
We stand on your greatness,
balanced in all directions,
complete in all that you are.*

III.

LEADING WITH LOVE

*When we tap the power within,
we realize that courage
is not limited to
what happens on the outside
but to the truth within,
always leading us
from the illusion of fear
with the eternal light of love.*

• CHAPTER 10 •

Lead

*Inclusion seeks authenticity over perfection,
appreciates quirks over strengths,
cultivates comfort with discomfort,
connects synergy with success,
builds the unseen,
decrees the unspoken,
adapts as well as focuses,
serves as well as leads.*

The power of inclusion is in leadership. Leadership is not limited to a role or title conveyed by someone else. We are all leaders. We are all blessed with opportunities to share our vision and be a light to others. We will all have times that we are called upon to make decisions to use what we learned. We all have to lead ourselves through the wilderness of experiences that will be the catalyst of our growth. Leadership is not only what we have to teach but also what we must be taught.

Excellent leadership does not cower in the convenience of people and experiences we are comfortable with but connects with the unknown and uncomfortable to do what we have never done, be who we have never been, and experience what we have never experienced. We are not effective leaders unless we are courageous enough to listen to others and respect that they might have something to share that is better than we ever imagined.

The most difficult people to lead are ourselves.

Inclusion tests our resilience. We stand on the values of our ancestors but also on the weakness of their mistakes. They led us to this moment of believing we could create perfection for ourselves by seeing imperfection in others. They built a world of hatred, shame, violence, greed, unworthiness, and animosity, gifting us with its legacy. Inclusion is a way out, an opening of truth that allows us to see beyond fear. We have enough. We are enough. We are here to support all of our relations, to lead beyond the limitations of our past. Excellent leadership begins from within. When we know that our purpose does not serve us but the greater good, we can't help but be inclusive. Inclusive leaders are proactive about allowing everyone to share their diverse perspectives, experiences, and ideas.

Excellent leadership is the power that uplifts the good in everyone.

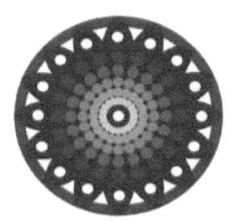

*Inclusive leaders create opportunity
to recognize the gifts of all participants.
This is an opportunity to circle with praise.
If you role-model your ability to see the greatness
in others, those who follow your leadership
will do the same.*

*If you have team meetings in circle,
which is a good practice for listening to everyone,
open with an expression of appreciation
in your own words of praise,
or uplift the strength of the team's power
with a poem, a quote, or a meditation
like the following:*

*"You are the light, the power, and the glory
that moves us forward with power, peace,
and purpose right now.
Nothing can stop you from achieving your greatness.
You can't lose with what you use.
You are in your right place, at your appointed time,
stepping into your greatness.*

*This is your season,
and you will realize the unlimited potential
and endless possibility of all that victory is."*

*Revisit circle rules as necessary:
Only speak when you have the Talking Piece.
The Talking Piece moves in one direction.
You can pass the piece in silence.
Speak from your own experience.*

*Prompts should be vehicles for recognizing
the contributions of everyone on the team:
"If you could lift up the greatness
of each one of your team members,
what would you say?"*

Framework for Leadership

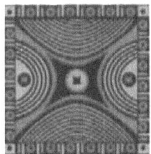

We cannot discuss inclusion without mentioning the practical steps of a framework for leading an organization willing to become more diverse, equitable, accessible, and inclusive. If you are not ready to become more diverse, inclusive, accessible, and equitable, you will eventually find yourself subjected to the legal requirement and oversight that will help provide a foundation for your readiness. At some point, some of us will lead the rudimentary work required to build the foundation of a diverse, equitable, accessible, and inclusive environment. The evolving landscape for a framework will be determined by the culture and core values of the environment.

Our Census alone shows that we cannot ignore the diversity that makes up the world. The U.S. Census and other research statistics show that as of 2020, there were approximately 250 million people racialized as White in the U.S. There were over 61 million people who reported in the 2019 census as Hispanic. Over 53 million people in the U.S. are racialized as Black, including those who describe themselves as part-Black, as most, if not all, Black people are multiracial. There were over 20 million listed as Asian, Native Hawaiian, and Other Pacific Islanders. Over 4 million are listed in the census as American Indian or Native Alaskan, a heart-breaking number for us all, deprived of those who are indigenous to this land. At a minimum, the percentages reflecting our population should be reflected in the workplace.

Twenty-seven of the 100 largest metropolitan areas have populations with BIPOC is in the majority, including New York, Los Angeles, Washington, D.C., Miami, Dallas, Atlanta, and Orlando. More than half of the nation's population under age 16 identifies as a racial or ethnic minority. Among this group, Latinx and Black residents together comprise nearly 40% of the population. In 24 years, by 2045, White people will be in the minority in the U.S. Worldwide, African and Asian countries will have the greatest growth.

Notwithstanding the difficulty expressed by some people about finding suitable candidates of color, diversifying the workplace is the easy part. Diversity is also more easily tracked and can be established through goals, efforts, and achievements represented by quantitative data. The more challenging task is to create an environment that is welcoming and inclusive, where everyone feels as though they belong and have equitable opportunities and tools to succeed. The question for leaders is what organizational core values support goals for a welcoming, inclusive environment? Do you have organizational core values to create a common ground for supporting everyone?

Excellent leadership inspires commitment.

THE POWER OF INCLUSION

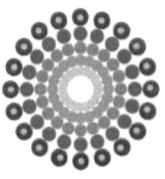

*Racism is inherent in every work culture
in the United States.*

*If you don't believe that,
then you are in denial and need a harsh reality check
from someone courageous enough
to give you their honest opinion.
Hopefully, no one wants to be oblivious to the pain
ignorance causes others.*

*George Floyd's daughter said
my daddy changed the world,
and she is correct.*

*It's the first time in a long time
that White people opened their eyes
wide enough to witness the racism
that is everywhere present because they could not ignore
Chavin's murder of Floyd.*

*Take a moment, and read the accounts
of all of the Black people*

murdered by police over the last few months,
or the violence against the AAPI community,
or the suffering of the Latinx community,
or the genocide of those indigenous
to this land by White people.

Think about your own circle of friends
and close-knit colleagues: do they
reflect someone from all of these groups?

I read through a book on inclusive leadership
and the word racism was mentioned only twice,
once to suggest that the term "micro-aggression"
was preferred, which actually undermines
the significance of the continued perpetration of assaults.

When was the last time you called a BIPOC colleague and
asked them how they were coping with the challenges
in their lives? When was the last time you sponsored and
fought for a Black person to be hired?
When was the last time you recognized the contributions
of those who look different than you?

Commitment and Baseline

You have to be committed—mind, body, and soul to DEAI. Otherwise, your efforts will not activate the full power of inclusion. The baseline, an examination of where you are in your organizational efforts to be diverse, equitable, accessible, and inclusive, will give you an idea of what you are committed to change as well as the struggles that are inherent on your journey.

The only way to create an inclusive environment is for the organization's leadership to be committed to its creation and everything necessary to accomplish this cultural change. Regardless of whether you are an enterprise, industry, government, partnership, collective institute, or network of broadcasters, filmmakers or other forms of entertainment, a hospital, pharmaceutical or medical service, a law firm, defense or prosecutorial organization, a government agency or branch, a corporation, partnership, cohort, or other business entity, it is important to ask how you can improve. Related to the question of improvement is how inclusion can help you achieve your goals? What is your history? How can you learn from your failures and success? What are the deep roots of any resistance to change? How can your recognition of failures contribute to a new commitment to change?

Commitment requires the establishment of a baseline for transparency, contrast, and goal-setting. What are your demographics in your overall population for all areas of your organization? You can simply look at who is in your organization and what they do, and the story tells itself. You need these stats to determine your baseline for improvement.

Is the organization willing to do whatever is necessary and stay the course to create a more diverse, equitable, accessible, and inclusive environment? The goals to create change do not happen overnight; it is an involved process. Are you willing to dig deep enough to ask the question and be accountable for whatever issues have caused people to feel "less than"? This is uncomfortable work. Will you be committed to finding and listening to whatever voices are missing? Deep listening is required. Will you not only invite those who are missing from the table but keep them there? Influencing key stakeholders requires creativity. Are you and your key stakeholders committed to implementing change regardless of what it takes? In addition to demographics, what are your hiring practices, promotional and advancement practices, programs, pipeline development, internships, stretch opportunities, etc.? Do you reflect the country's demographics in all aspects of your operations? Who comprises your board and staff?

Excellent leadership discovers what is wrong and commits to manifesting what is right.

Diverse Stakeholders

You have to have a diverse team committed to accomplishing your DEAI goals, a team that can provide diverse perspectives, input, and analysis to lead, plan and implement. Whoever you are discussing as the recipient of what you are planning should be represented in the discussions. If you don't have the benefit of someone else's experience, you cannot represent them. It doesn't matter if you are married to someone of a certain background or ethnic group. If you have not had their experience, then you cannot provide the benefit of their insight. Science clearly supports that the more diverse the input, the more innovative the outcome.

Excellent leadership values all perspectives.

Vision, Mission, and Goals

In addition to commitment and creating a baseline for starting your efforts, you must define what success looks like for you. Otherwise, you will not be able to establish that you have made a movement towards that success. This requires creating a vision, which is aspirational; a mission, which you expect to accomplish as part of your long-term plan; and goals, which are concrete steps towards completing your mission while adhering to the power of your vision.

Excellent leadership develops vision, mission, and goals as the centerpiece of a strategic plan.

Inclusive Culture Strategy

You need to create an inclusive culture strategy that encompasses your core values and provides a catalyst for operational support and a strategy that will improve the organization by embracing the importance of its accomplishments for everyone and every operational goal. There should be a story and a cultural theme that mid-level leadership can attest to as well. You have to ask what your values are? How does inclusion help achieve your objectives as an organization? What slogans are already used that support inclusion? One of the best ways to gain additional insight into your workforce and build a bond around inclusive culture goals is to retreat and share ideas by brainstorming about the issues. If the organization is large, you may need to take several months to receive the leadership's input by hearing from all leaders possible, which is of critical importance, so it is worth the time spent. This is not merely a "listening tour"; it is strategic planning, educating for accountability, and cultivating partners for support.

Excellent leadership develops an inclusive culture strategy.

CECILIA B. LOVING

Partners Supporting Accountability

There will be resistance to DEAI goals in every organization, as well as supportive partners to help push the needle for progress. Some partners may appear adversarial, applying pressure both within and outside the organization, but they still support change. The latter include government agencies or offices requiring status reports, evaluations, or audits; foundations, boards, and clients who pay for services and demand change; legal authorities, decisions and/or monitors; affiliated organizations, employee resource groups, internal compliance systems; and those who make it their business to keep you informed. These partners provide opportunities for creating reliable systems to survey, track and keep tabs on accomplishments and areas for improvement, including key stakeholders and their attention to DEAI goals. Every challenge, crisis, and opposition is an opportunity to bring about necessary change.

Excellent leadership uses every challenge to achieve success.

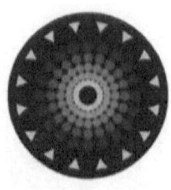

Strategic Plan and Annual Reporting

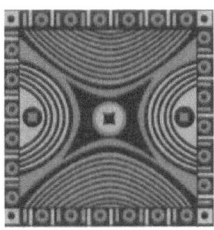

Your strategic plan should be based on your Inclusive Culture Strategy. Your strategic plan requires that you plan with agility, adjusting as necessary. Be patient with yourself. This plan is a process that will depend on what you want to measure, report, message, and encourage. Your plan is not just to organize your thoughts but also to galvanize your success. Your plan is an opportunity to honor those who have contributed and those you hope will contribute to your DEAI goals in the future. Your plan is an opportunity to praise those champions to the cause, as well as the unsung heroes.

Your plan should highlight both your internal and external accomplishments. How can you organize your accomplishments to show their relationship with what is important to your organizational DEAI goals? For example, have you partnered with outside organizations? The plan provides an opportunity to establish how your work with them supports your in-house objectives. For example, if there is a Gender Equity Commission or a Taskforce on Racial Inclusion and Equity that you have collaborated with, the plan provides a platform for those initiatives and structure for future initiatives.

If you have a well-defined inclusive culture strategy, you should be able to allocate all of your goals with each tenet for what you hope to accomplish. Create a timeline for your journey, showing where you have been and the trajectory of where you need to go. Share awards, successes, resources, and measurements establishing your accomplishments. In addition to setting forth what you would like to accomplish and why your goals are important to the creation of a more positive and holistic workplace, include the testimonials of those who have benefited from programs.

Similar to the strategic plan, also tell your story through an annual report. This is your platform for history, education, truth-telling, and inspiration. Do not wait for anyone to tell you to report on what has been accomplished. You will be pleasantly surprised that you have done far more than you imagined. The more you share your story with others, the more accountable you will be to its success. Create a tradition of periodic reporting. Using the same approach provides a framework that can be continued regardless of who leads DEAI in the future.

Excellent leadership tells the story of success,
while managing expectations,
planning change with ample time to grow.

Education

One of the most important things my friend, colleague, and mentor in the DEAI space, CDIO Anna Brown, shared with me is never to stop educating myself. DEAI is a growing field that constantly creates and redefines itself. Moreover, DEAI is an intersection of several different social sciences, artistic, legal, and spiritual fields. Educate yourselves continuously regarding DEAI. Several certified DEAI courses, including one given by the Cornell University School of Industrial and Labor Relations, and the Yale University School of Management, can be used. Avail yourself of all resources.

Education is not limited to reading; most, if not all DEAI leaders, are eager to speak with you as well. One of my colleagues, Gina Leow, and I contacted as many CDIOs as who would speak with us, and from them, we learned some of our most valuable lessons. There is no room for withholding secrets. We learn from each other, honoring our responsibility to give back.

Our education begins with examining ourselves. We all have to reflect on our knowledge, biases, and blind spots. If we cannot find adequate resources, we must create them. Unconscious bias, LGBTQ, sexual harassment, EEO, allyship, emotional intelligence, religious diversity, disability etiquette, and racial inclusion training is part of an ongoing curriculum.

DEAI education is ongoing for all as we grow to understand one another. This is uncomfortable work; it triggers the soul. But we have to be comfortable with being uncomfortable. Education is what helps us process how to improve our relationship with ourselves as well as others.

Creating internal DEAI Training Units helps ensure that education evolves as part of the culture and provides instruction by those who understand the work environment and apply the training to their experience. This training can be done live or virtually, through videos, webinars, virtual books, or infographics—all of which tell stories, provide introspection, and result in teachable moments for lasting change.

Excellent leadership knows that education is not the only step in maintaining an inclusive culture but is an indispensable one.

Messaging

Storytelling is an essential part of DEAI. As the late Paul Robeson said, *art is power; it affects politics and brings about change.*

I have several paintings on my walls at home, but the one I love the most was painted by an artist named George Hunt, who said a blind man once told him, "paint something I can see." I can close my eyes and run my hands across the painting, and feel the raised texture of fabric. I can touch the painting and feel the cigarette burn in a hat and the hair in a mustache. Making that painting accessible was profound. Hunt created an artistic experience that is available to those who need to touch it to see it, as well as for those who can use their eyesight. The messages inherent in artistic expression raise consciousness, build trust, enhance authenticity, and provide the courage to create lasting change.

Deafblind lawyer and activist Haben Girma says those with different abilities create opportunities for growth and innovation. The best way to realize our common ground and respect and include each other is through the power of our stories, so we have to enlist our best storytellers and leaders who offer the greatest genius for innovation.

Innovation labs are a great way to support creativity, which can be done in a one-day retreat or longer. You create an agenda and activities that support camaraderie, a safe space for creativity, and collaboration for the most productive ideas.

As a result, messaging in all of its various forms—posters, books, videos, infographics, cards, screensavers, vignettes, drama, cards, animation, games, play, dance, song, music, talks, poetry, visual art—all bring about change. Our institutions that provide powerful mediums of expression have an added advantage of truthtelling. For example, broadcasting companies, museums, and other cultural institutions are considered to safeguard the truth and are sanctuaries of our experiences. Data shows that people revere them; they are more trusted than any other source of information and are among the best educational assets we have. They can be leaders in DEAI because they have unique social capital. When I witness the genius of Kehinde Wiley, Amy Tan, Lin-Manual Miranda, Amy Karl, or visit the Charles Wright Museum in Detroit and see the slave ship reenacted or the power of any other art, the message is clearer, deeper, vivid, and more lasting.

Excellent leadership realizes the value of innovation and the power of storytelling.

Committees, Taskforces, Advocates, and Messaging Units

Additional systems of education, accountability, support, messaging, and leadership committed to DEAI are supported by diversity councils or committees comprised of key stakeholders and voices essential to be heard. Councils or committees should have Charters, setting forth a statement of their goals, leadership, members, sub-committees, and other attributes. Similarly, taskforces should be formed to address issues on a short-term basis, providing focused action plans, root cause analysis, and possible results. Diversity and/or Inclusion Advocates can be used to advocate, champion, message, teach, counsel, and hold space for the improvement of DEAI. Communications Strategists and Mobile Messaging Units created from the employees in the work culture can help improve and disseminate the DEAI message in other locations throughout the organization.

Excellent leadership never stops building a community of stakeholders.

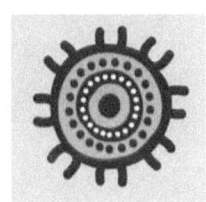

Results

For accountability, we have to create a culture that wants the data and realizes its importance. We need to promote transparency, confront our assumptions, start with where we want to end, and from that vantage point, monitor our success. Whether it's recruitment stats, climate surveys, focus groups, feedback surveys, testimonials, or other systems of accountability, the evidence is a vital way to tell the truth about what has taken place and what has the potential to be done. Equity and Results is a powerful organization that teaches how to account for success using a root cause analysis and a racial equity focus.

Excellent leadership realizes that
measuring results energizes momentum.

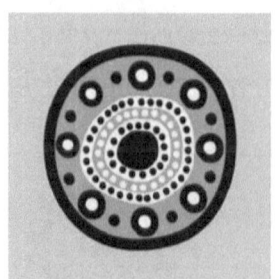

Inclusive Leadership Skills

A Chief Diversity and Inclusion Officer is essential to lead the goals of DEAI, but one person is not enough. The entire organization is accountable, especially the person or people leading the organization in the C-Suite. When a CDIO fails, it is not because the individual in the role failed; it is because the organization itself did so. It is easy to scapegoat someone else because leadership failed to rally around the CDIO and support the goals of DEAI.

Similarly, when a CDIO succeeds, the entire organization has worked hard to move the needle toward success and turn the curve toward lasting change. Every step is essential on this journey without end. A concerted effort and a critical mass of support are imperative. The CDIO must report to the head of the organization. Otherwise, there is a significant risk that the CDIO's ideas will be diminished by the additional layer of supervision—whether intentional or not. Even those supportive of DEAI have their own agendas, which may impact the CDIO's ability to do their job. The issues confronted by a CDIO are challenging, which would be complicated by a third party or intercessory.

A CDIO is set up to fail if they are not provided with administrative support. At a minimum, they need a small team. A CDIO cannot do everything. They need administrative, creative, legal, and managerial support and a devoted team of champions providing their ideas, creativity, and understanding of the culture. For example, some organizations provide the CDIO with a Director, Manager, Coordinator, and Communications Strategist. With some creativity, a DEAI Training Unit, DEAI Champions, Circle-keepers, and many others can be added to the team.

When we lead with integrity, vision, and the requisite support, we have a better opportunity to succeed in accomplishing some goals on this journey without end. The 21st Century should be able to end racism or any other form of discrimination. Class divisions should become distant memories of the past because, like race, the superiority of rank and title are constructs. The truth is that none of us is better than anyone else. True achievement should be based on what we give rather than what we take.

How we lead ourselves will determine how we lead others. If we cannot lead ourselves, we will not be effective in leading others. Authenticity, appreciation, and adaptiveness are the cornerstones of an excellent leader.

The CDIO is not the only person who must exhibit excellent leadership; all leaders must do so.

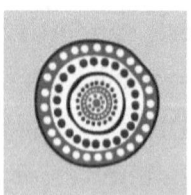

Authentic Leadership

A senior partner's office was next door to mine at one of the law firms where I worked. He walked in the door as I sat at the desk wearing my new Brooks Brothers suit with a pleated skirt and traditional cream-colored blouse. He was quick, forthright, deliberate, impatient, brilliant. "Where did you clerk?" he asked, as though my answer to that question would determine my fate —or at least give him a yardstick by which to measure me. As far as he was concerned, all lawyers at the firm clerked with a federal judge. The firm's first Black female associate, who recruited me, had clerked.

"I didn't clerk," I answered, "I worked at Legal Aid." I was sure my answer to that question would resign me to what I perceived as my inevitable fate to fend for myself. But that was an easy way out that this authentic leader had no interest in taking. I graduated from a top ten law school, where I served as the first Black Managing Editor of one of its journals. I was one of five Black attorneys out of 130 to work at Legal Aid, also recruited there by another Black lawyer. I was good enough, or they wouldn't have hired me. But I was different.

He didn't miss a beat. He described his own prestigious background, clerking with the most prestigious jurists, including some

U.S. Supreme Court Justices. He had the most prestigious resume I had ever encountered then, and even until this day. But his grace and generosity were equally impressive. He was not there to disparage me but find common ground and give me the benefit of his privilege. He became what I would recognize many years later as my sponsor.

A sponsor is more than a mentor. A sponsor doesn't just show you the ropes, take you to lunch and offer you a few pieces of good advice. A sponsor fights for you, lobbies on your behalf, gets you the best assignments, and teaches you the right way. A sponsor is your strongest advocate, especially when you're not in the room. A sponsor anoints you.

The funny thing is, I don't ever recall my sponsor and I going to lunch as typical mentors and mentees do. But my sponsor did more than give me a free meal. He rubbed my life with the holy oil of relevancy, capability, credibility, and legacy. I mattered to his partners because he said I mattered. He used his own privilege to establish whatever I lacked in the eyes of others. Instead of undermining my Legal Aid background, he touted it for what it was, a great experience, with complete autonomy as a lawyer. As a junior associate, I had already argued more cases in New York Appellate Court than his own colleagues. While others were clerking, I was making a difference in the lives of indigent clients who could not afford counsel.

He chose to see the good in me, something that more elitist eyes would never fathom. Young White men are anointed all the time—not because they are smarter or better, but simply because someone else says they are. We judge people by what other people say about them. Instead of allowing people to show up as their authentic selves, most try to force them into a shoe that doesn't fit. I succeeded under his sponsorship for the simple reason that he accepted me as I was. He understood the power of an anointing, having someone credible say that you are worthy. Generally, only those who are White get the best assignments in a law firm.

My sponsor understood one of the most important principles of inclusion—our ability to anoint others, brand them as the best person ever, as someone who should be given every opportunity, tool, resource, and experience to succeed. I've used this approach to sponsor others ever since. He said I tell my partners that you will always have come from this firm no matter what you decide to do.

He gave me a legacy that I had been without. He may not have realized that I was a Black woman born and raised in Detroit in a community struggling with drug addiction, prostitution, jail, and teenage pregnancy. But he accepted me as I was: strong, smart, tough, and resilient, and he added the firm's privilege. When I chose to leave, the firm's credibility helped open new doors.

My sponsor had something more than a prestigious resume; he had the gift of emotional intelligence and the insight of an authentic leader. He knew who he was and how to regulate his communications with me to make it safe for me to make mistakes and learn a great deal. He also knew how to advocate with integrity, fairness, humility, and transparency.

The essential EQ skills include three self-management skills: self-awareness, self-regulation, and pro-social behavior. When you are emotionally intelligent, you are curious. You are flexible and accommodating. You are aware of emotional triggers and how to navigate them. You are empathetic and respect the boundaries of others. You know how to release a grudge and divert chaos to find common ground. You know how to balance work and rest.

High-EQ individuals take people's opinions with a grain of salt. Instead, they form their own opinions, knowing that self-worth comes from within. Authentic leaders are guided by compassion for others. They are not divisive or controlling bullies. Instead, they are engaged and supportive, empowering their subordinates and building lasting relationships with their colleagues.

I share this story because we often talk about environments that are not inclusive across color lines and gender. But we need to know what inclusive behavior looks like. Because I was sponsored, I became a sponsor for countless others. My sponsor's legacy not only benefitted me but generations to come. Those I helped also helped others. When you have a sponsor as your advocate, you can show up as your best self, and you can take the necessary risk to share new ideas because someone believes in you. An authentic leader respects who you are, using the best that you are to make your case. An authentic leader embraces differences as a strength and does not try to make someone fit a mold but step into the light of who they are as a benefit to everyone.

How authentic are you as a leader?
Who have you given the benefit of your privilege
by uplifting their authenticity?
Have you anointed people who look different than you?
How can you support the authenticity of those who are different?

Appreciative Leadership

Leadership is complicated by the trauma we suffer. It cannot be over-emphasized that to have the capacity to lead with an appreciation of others, we have to first take care of ourselves. The need to embrace others with compassion applies to everyone regardless of their racial construct. For example, Black people may accept the authenticity of their Black colleagues and still fail to show appreciation for them. In his book *BRAINWASHED: Challenging the Myth of Black Inferiority*, Tom Burrell discusses "crabbing" and "backstabbing," the intense jealousy and contempt that some Black people have for other Black people.

Burrell says "crabbing" is the desire to keep someone from achieving. While "backstabbing" is jealousy, envy, and hateful behavior in an attempt to sabotage another's success. This painful reality is one of many underlying traumas that we all need to deal with to uplift each other and transform our attitude into a positive and supportive one. As Burrell says, "don't hate, elevate." Inclusion does not just apply to one demographic. Inclusion should be taken seriously *within* all demographic groups.

In Native American tradition, there is a saying of gratitude to uplift appreciation as "the words that come before all else." When we call "all our relations" into the energy of appreciation, we know that there is enough for everyone and everything to be revered. Competition is fear based on an erroneous interpretation of the universe as being limited in supply. But the truth is that there is enough happiness for everyone. We don't need to dim our lights or stop ourselves from being too bright, too happy, too successful, too visible, too unusual, too vivid, too loud, too different, *too much*.

We should not have to worry about haters who seek to marginalize us when we are being our best. We need to work on releasing any hatred, disagreement, or discord. We need to sing our song, dance our dance, speak our speech, take our stand, and stay our course because that's why we are here. We need to stop limiting ourselves because of other people's opinions. Let us not deprive ourselves, the universe, or, most importantly, others of all that we can be.

Everyone's goal is to make sure that no one feels excluded. For some, it may be easier to show an interest in cultures other than your own. But you also need to support those who look like you. When you see a coworker in need of a word of encouragement, encourage them. Pay a thoughtful compliment. Never discount the power of your words. Words alone are a vehicle for change. Watch the nasty narratives that you circulate to try to undermine someone else's greatness. Any attempts to undermine someone else simply undermines you. Refrain from gossip, ridicule, bragging, and disrespect.

In his book *Choosing Civility*, P.M. Forni says some people believe they will shine if we make others look bad. It is less demanding and less painful to point out other people's problems—real or imaginary—than to solve our own. We should praise others, which actually makes us feel better. What we give always comes back. A growth mindset starts with a belief in our shared potential.

The following is a list of ways we can be more inclusive:

1. *Communicate with transparency.* Refrain from using information and knowledge as a way to exclude others.
2. *Behave consistently.* Try to navigate your own emotional rollercoaster so that it does not upset or confuse others. Moods undermine our credibility and the trust that we need from our leaders.
3. *Show a sincere interest in the aspirations and goals of others.* Don't just ask questions and listen; try to think of ways you can assist with the accomplishment of someone else's goals. You will be surprised by just how helpful you can be.
4. *Take responsibility for both failures as well as successes.* A leader's integrity is essential. Everyone makes mistakes; the goal is to minimize them and to be honest if they are made.
5. *Communicate respectfully.* Leaders have a high standard to be respectful in tone, reaction, and when reporting incidents. We should not bully or attempt to undermine someone by creating a negative narrative.
6. *Use check-ins, visits, praise reports, show and tells, and circles.* Get to know each other and learn what's important to as many people as possible. Meetings and lunches, whether virtual or not, go a long way in establishing meaningful connections.
7. *Keep your word.* At a minimum, do what you say you will do, and aim to do more. The only way to move the needle is to do the work, but give yourself more than enough time to accomplish what needs to be done.
8. *Be a catalyst for action.* Share the truth and be proactive about

tapping resources to engage and improve.

9. *See the best in the others.* People want to be around those who make them feel good about themselves rather than those who are toxic.

10. *Be an ally.* Learn the histories of those who have been oppressed and support their cause as much as your own. When one person suffers, we all do.

Appreciative leaders turn creative potential into positive power. Everyone has potential that is just waiting to be recognized. The most appreciative leaders have a radar for potential that they recognize when others do not. They let people know they are valued. They bring out the best. They provide opportunities. They inspire and awaken creative energy. They provide a sense of direction and integrity. They recognize the best, and they give the same. Appreciative leaders share positive narratives and allow all to tell their stories to build connection, realizing stories hold culture, co-create reality, and build bridges of appreciation.

Do you make appreciation a part of your interaction with everyone, focusing on the positive rather than the negative?

Adaptive Leadership

Adaptive leaders are nimble, flexible, realizing that things are constantly changing. They tap all available resources to create change through innovation. They encourage trust, transparency, and communication. Adaptive leaders can lead as well as be led with equal proficiency. They realize all mentoring relationships are reciprocal. They love technology and expect their colleagues to be creative, team-oriented, respectful, as well as independent. Humility is a vital attribute of adaptive leadership. Adaptive leaders incorporate the rapidly changing landscape around them. They are not afraid to be vulnerable, to reveal that there are things they do not know, that they are not perfect.

Adaptive leaders realize the need to collaborate, inspire, and unite what appears to be fractions to create a collective whole. They support transformation by creating a safe space to hold the diverse views of others and to encourage difficult conversations. They are flexible in establishing the goals and milestones for any task. They provide a support network to bring about change through the organization from grassroots, top, and middle.

Adaptive leaders are strategic. They evaluate information carefully and vet the requisite response thoroughly. They realize the importance of navigating between the details and the big picture.

They know how to assess what is happening and take corrective action on more immediate concerns, as well as greater dynamics. They recognize that the struggle for change will be continuous but will also offer growth and strength. The change that organizations seek to be more inclusive will also require changes within their leaders: both are dependent on the other.

Adaptive leaders know that they will not be able to make everyone happy. To get the best out of their colleagues, adaptive leaders realize the importance of staying on target and guiding those they lead out of their comfort zones. Sometimes they have to exercise tough love for teachable moments, stay on course, address and minimize mistakes, and do what's best for the organization. Influence is key.

An adaptive leader knows how to influence change through competence, commitment, creativity, compassion, communication, and courage. Courage isn't necessarily loud and aggressive. Courage can be constant, methodical, tactical, consistent, and patient, realizing that change rarely happens overnight. An adaptive leader is a loving leader who knows the importance of putting others first.

What is your vision for the organization?
How do you message it in all that you do?
Does it captivate, motivate, encourage, and inspire?

· CHAPTER 11 ·

Begin

*Inclusion is beginning
wherever we are,
not merely hoping for a new day,
but doing whatever needs to be done
right now.*

It is imperative that we begin now, no longer waiting for someone else to do what needs to be done. In the sixties, we sang, "We shall overcome. We shall overcome . . . one day." Now is the time to overcome whatever stands in the way of good. If we need support, we need to be supportive. If we need someone to hear us, we need to listen. If we need violence to stop, we need to stop being violent. If we need some love, we need to be loving. If we need truth, we need to be honest. If we want liberation, we need to start by liberating ourselves. If we want inclusion, we need to be inclusive now—not just "one day."

We cannot expect the beloved community to emerge from the ethers without expressing through us. As a kid in the '60s, I wondered when the revolution would come; in the 21st century, I realize that the revolution is here. We are not simply the change we seek; we are the full potential and the greatest possibility of love there is. We have to be courageous enough to mirror what we would like to see in the world. We have to use whatever gifts and talents we have to move beyond our comfort zones and confront the ingrained racism and the self-absorbed privilege that prevents the world from honoring all beings. Inclusion does not ask what the world has in store for it but decrees what it has in store for the world.

What fears are you holding onto? Inclusion is the catalyst through which you release them. What animosity do you carry? Inclusion is the alchemy that delivers you from whatever resentments you harbor. We are all suffering from the trauma of the ignorance and greed of our ancestors. Inclusion challenges us to heal our pain and be supportive of the healing of others. The only way to liberate ourselves is to be vulnerable, humble, empathetic, and compassionate. The only way to build a world of love is to give it.

Are you a gatekeeper, hiding behind the cowardice of trying to control someone else? Are you a bully using shame to feel superior? Do you gossip to create a narrative that demeans someone else because that is the story you choose to tell? Do you spend time in social media confined to the drama of illusion instead of building an inclusive ecosystem for the entire planet?

Michele Obama said, "when they go low, we go high." Going "high" requires spiritual energy. Going "high" allows us to tap into that part of us that is pure Spirit. Going high is recognizing the positive power that we are, a power that stands on the shoulders of the unseen to be a supernatural force for good.

We have wallowed in the trauma of our ancestors, but now is time to stand on the shoulders of their strength. What gave them the bravery, the honor, the preparation, the dedication, the ability, the willingness to give their all? Spirit. It is time to tap the same Spirit that guided them and let a new earth be born in us. We are all called to perform a service to humanity, make us better than we were before, and use our gifts and talents to help everyone—not just those who look like us. Anger serves its purpose to motivate, energize, and encourage, but we are stagnated by it if we stay bitter for too long.

Our goal is to lead ourselves with patience, wisdom, and compassion by building bridges that will provide meaningful and transformational connections throughout the world. By listening, engaging, and exchanging with those whose ideas are different than our own, we stretch beyond the familiar to see through a different lens and create more beneficial solutions by achieving what is best for everyone. We have the power to create the world we live in, but the more we fantasize about its destruction through myths centered on weakness, hatred, and violence, the more we create lower vibrations that lead to those scenarios. It is time to write a different script.

Being able to embrace everyone with compassion, heal ourselves, strengthen our leadership, and rise with the co-creative power of renewal flips the script of worry, doubt, and fret to vision, voice, and victory. *Now*, the portal to the future is open and welcomes us as the gateway to move beyond bitterness and resentment to peace and harmony. We are our own heroes, gifted with the superpowers that we need to triumph. We cannot wait for anyone but ourselves to lead us into a new world. Now is the time to toss the Hollywood horror script of destruction and instead be the victory of a good story for everyone.

Take a moment to center in the power of what you can begin
to do to help others rather than hurt them.
How can you contribute to the movement
of a better life for all people
and a healthier existence on our planet?
What can you do to foster a more positive work environment?
Think of what results you want to achieve
right now.
Welcome everyone necessary
to help you achieve those goals.

Vision

One of the best things that we can do for ourselves is to open our eyes and see what is right before us, and envision what we have the power to mold and shape. We can see with the physical eye, like revering those things around us and appreciating those things we see as we travel physically or virtually. My mother has a fantastic ability to revere the things around her. In the days when she and my dad would visit New York City and could walk the long blocks in Brooklyn, she would be in awe of everything—things I often took for granted. She would marvel at every garden that we walked past in Carroll Gardens, breathing in their sweet fragrance and enjoying the magnificence of their colorful blossoms. She would recall what she planted that season or what she had planted in the past. It was a slow, delicious walk—meant to absorb, marvel, and be fully present.

I recall a trip to the East Village, when my mother went into every shop, every hole in the wall, every nook and cranny, and eyed every vendor's display of goods in awe. She saw their artistry with every aspect of her being and breathed in their fragrances of incense, curry, and sage. She had jewelry made for her un-pierced ears. She spoke to every craftsperson, every artist, and discovered things I never knew. She enjoyed what was there in a single block—that I would have raced past.

In the same way, we rush through our environments, we also rush through people and their differences that we can be in awe of, those we often take for granted. Every second gives us something to marvel at. If we revered each other, we would see and respect each other in a new way. Then, we can look deeply into the experiences of who we are and how they vary and fully appreciate all that we each bring to this world. We may have missed each other during the pandemic, but the experience of being locked in should teach us how to see each other with more humility and gratitude.

Awe, the ability to revere and appreciate others brings us happiness, which ignites our souls and heals our bodies. Many of us use social media for awe rather than appreciate what is in the world around us. We have to look up from our virtual spaces and open new windows in our souls that see the world and all our relations in a new way. How can we love, how can we appreciate others if we are so busy condemning, arguing, or resenting each other?

Scientists have discovered that our ability to uplift others makes us healthier. We are here to enjoy the world—here to be in the presence of life and experience its beauty in a new way. But do we even see or know our neighbors? Do we see beyond our Netflix and our text messages to really enjoy the meals we photograph, see the color and feel the texture of the experience we live in? When we see and appreciate what is around us, we not only connect with life differently, but we develop more empathy and respect for each other. Who will you see today? How will you welcome and connect with them in a manner that makes them feel as though they belong?

We are also able to envision beyond the physical, which is a power available to all of us, and it is this vision that allows us to create a better world, one in which we are welcoming of everyone, one in which we all belong, and most importantly—one where we are all valued. Our creative power has several dimensions, part of which is the power to envision, imagine, and be open and receptive to infinite ideas. Through creativity, we can release doubt or worry and trust in our ability to co-create by setting goals, acquiring new skills, addressing challenges, and moving beyond self-imposed limitations.

Take a moment and breathe in a new awareness
of your power of vision. See what is before you.
Envision your dreams and give shape to their reality.
Release whatever and whoever no longer serves you.
Release your ties to people who are triggers.
Let go of the burdens you saw in your past,
and see instead what you would love to see
and how you would like the world to be.

We can see with the vision of Rosa Parks. How many times had she taken that bus and walked to the back when she was tired. She released her fear and took a seat. She saw past the status quo to the courage she needed to help change the world. She tapped her superpower of vision, and so did the civil rights leaders working with her.

We can see with the faith of Harriet Tubman. How many times had she been beaten? How many times had she been treated like an animal? How many times had she watched her family suffer until she tapped the creative power within? Yet, she stood in the cold, harsh weather, a beacon of light for those who needed her to guide them through the underground railroad. With her vision, she returned to harm's way, again and again, a warrior of freedom embodied as the soul of a former enslaved African. Vision is a powerful gift that we share.

We can see with the genius of Fannie Lou Hammer. How many times had she wanted to cast her vote? How many times had she suffered from not experiencing equal rights and justice before she stood up and said, "I'm sick and tired of being sick and tired"? She was fired for casting her ballot, lost property, and suffered the threats of the terrorists who have long invaded this country disguised as supremacy. Because of her vision, her voice was heard, and institutions were formed, improving the lives of millions.

There are many different ways to envision.

One of my favorites is the "projected diary," mentioned in Eric Butterworth's book *The Creative Life*. You simply write in a journal or diary what took place on the day before it happens, which you can do the evening of or the morning before. I have manifested things that I never thought I could do using the power of the projected diary.

Another tool to see beyond our current circumstances is to write a letter to the day, the week, the month, or even the year before it takes place. We can be as detailed as possible to really see and feel a sense of gratitude for what we desire to see take shape.

Another tool is a vision board of drawings and photographs of what we would like to see take place. Many take this tool a bit further and put the images on their monitor or post them in visible places in their homes.

I use my ability to envision every project that I work on, which allows me to use tools to create that I've never used before and engage people I have never worked with before. I'm always amazed at the success of the outcome. Seeing through the lens of success allows us to use our gifts of insight and imagination to co-create what we never thought possible.

*Project your day or your tomorrow,
or even your new year
to plant the seeds of change that need to take place.
Write an account of what
you would like to see take place
using the power of divine visualization—
as if it had already happened.
You can do this every day—
pushing beyond limitation
to an unlimited vision of success.*

Voice

We also can speak truth to power to see the changes that we want to see take place. We have the power to decree a thing and make it so. Every single word that we speak, whether it is silently to ourselves or out loud, every single utterance is speaking truth to power, so we need to watch what we say. We should not speak in a manner that undermines who we are, our purpose, our goals, or our vision because we can say a thing and make it so. We should not use our words to marginalize the success that we are. We should not utter that we are not good enough or "unworthy" because we are better than the best.

We need to turn off the monologues we have about doubt or lack. We cannot overemphasize the good that comes with saying great things about ourselves or decreeing what we desire to see take place. We are special; we are unique; we are divine. We can only get the best by expecting it. We must uplift the power of who we are. Whatever we speak of begins to take shape in the ethers.

Anger is essential to transforming what we no longer want to see, but it is equally important not to linger in it. We have to shift the paradigm of such a negative, harmful vibration, which lowers and slows down our ability to manifest what we desire, and instead of wallowing in it, we have to use it as a catalyst to energize the positive things we want to see take place.

We can use the power of our decrees to release what we no longer want to see or experience. Begin with decrees of denials. Denials are assertions of what will not take place in your life, what will not harm you. For example, "no one and nothing can keep my good from me" is a denial. "No weapon formed against me shall prosper" is a denial. "I release everyone, and everything which is not for my highest good" is a denial. "I am a child of God, and I do not inherit sickness" is a denial. It is believed that the universe abhors a vacuum, so denials clean out the unwanted thoughts and energy, but after we finish using denials, we must use affirmations to fill our creative consciousness with the new.

An affirmation is giving voice to what we want to see take place. There is no set way to write an affirmation, but certain rules will help provide a better understanding of what they are and the basics regarding how they should be structured. If you follow these guidelines to write your own affirmations and create empowering statements, there is no question that you will see the manifestation of your success from speaking them with power, boldness, and courage.

Be personal. Use "I," "me," and or your first name. Be positive.

Use the present tense. Command what you desire as though it has already taken place, using phrases like "I am"; "I have"; "I command." Quantum physicists say there is no such thing as time, so you can speak your truth as though it has already happened. For example, you can affirm, "The ideas that I need to accomplish what needs to be done reveal themselves swiftly." You can affirm, "The partners I need to help develop the changes that must be made help me—to do more than I could ever imagine, providing the support that results in our greatest good." You can always start by affirming the big picture: "Everything is working together for our good, in perfect, divine order." I am in my right place, at my right time. The universe conspires to help me.

Use action words that allow you to feel the emotion of what you desire to see take shape, like "I accomplish my good with ease" or "My cup runs over with success that gives me the joy and happiness of sharing my good with others." Feel and connect with the emotion you would have when receiving what you speak. Your consciousness responds to what you desire when saying affirmations with intent and purpose.

Never limit your desires. Let the power of your heart, mind, and soul reach for the stars. Recite your affirmations daily. Speak truth to power each day, preferably in the morning, by reciting your entire affirmation four times out loud. If you have time, follow your affirmation with a meditation.

When we affirm our best and highest state of consciousness, we bring that energy of positivity, courage, and success to every task we have, every relationship we form, and everything we do.

*Create an affirmation
for change you would
like to see in the world,
for the healing
that needs to take place.
Feel the emotion of achieving your goals.
Affirm the guidance and support
that you need to see
for all humanity.*

Victory

We are moving beyond compliance in DEAI as following human rights laws and equal employment opportunity policies and practices is a bare minimum for creating an environment that respects, honors, and uplifts everyone. Creating a positive and holistic world requires us to embody compassion and kindness in body, mind, and soul.

A genuine welcome does not force anyone to assimilate but welcomes their individuality as part of a collective whole with the potential to offer the gift of their unique experience and perspective. We share a gift when we experience different cuisines, art, language, clothing, hairdos, cultures, creeds, ages, and the creativity of different lifestyles. This does not mean that we should not respect the uniforms or safety precautions that our jobs may require, but it does mean that we should provide a safe space for the expression of our authentic selves. We cannot be our best selves unless we are authentic.

An inclusive mindset is a growth mindset, constantly learning, never fixed in one way to achieve results. An inclusive mindset and its resulting positivity respond to our core purpose to serve something greater than ourselves. When we receive an opportunity to succeed, our ability to improve the greater good is accelerated. When we give an opportunity to succeed, we are victorious before we even begin: the victory is in the act of building community by helping others.

A beloved community does the work necessary to eliminate exclusion, which subjects us to the same emotional stress as a neural impulse, as powerful and painful as a physical blow. We treat everyone with compassion, actively including so that we are not excluding. This does not mean that we can't take pride in our culture. Pride in who we are, especially for those of us from communities and cultures that have been marginalized, denigrated, and under-represented, should be uplifted in a manner that provides equity and honor.

I take pride in the fact that I attended what Ta-Nehisi Coates refers to as the "Mecca," Howard University, a historically Black University. Howard served as a powerful foundation for developing self-confidence, creativity, communication, compassion, and courage. Howard was a family that raised me so that when I entered other universities like UCLA, NYU, and New York Theological Seminary and the workplace at large, I could be my best. Education in an environment free of racism nurtures authenticity and provides the safest space for the confidence young people need to develop.

I also take pride in LGBT, Asian-Pacific, Hispanic, Jewish, Women, and other cultural events because of the power of pride that they encourage and the opportunities they give us to appreciate what is sacred in someone else's experience. Empathy heals us. Empathy is not a weakness but a strength that enhances our capabilities, relationships, and creativity.

THE POWER OF INCLUSION

When we create, we tap the inner power of the creator present in each one of us to contribute to the greater good. We are a conduit of divine ideas that must re-envision and redefine ourselves. As the Pulitzer Prize-winning Native American writer N. Scott Momaday wrote, "[w]e are what we imagine. Our very existence consists in our imagination of ourselves. Our best destiny is to imagine who and what and that we are. The greatest tragedy that can befall us is to go unimagined." Through this lens, we recognize the power of creativity in inclusion, that the doors should open—not just for us—but for everyone to be victorious.

*Create a project this month
that allows you to give to someone else.
Pour your heart into finishing it.
Wrap it in your finest paper.
Give to your soul the full experience
of making it special,
so wonderful you now want to keep it.
Then, give it away.*

• CHAPTER 12 •

Love

*Without love,
inclusion does not exist.*

Love is inclusion. Love embraces everyone as an extension of one family, realizing that when one suffers, we all suffer. This love is unconditional, pure love, not romance but the capacity to be kind, caring, and compassionate with one another, regardless of our differences.

We have spent a lot of energy in the last several decades focusing on diversity, but we have scarcely scratched the surface of inclusion. Our greater purpose in being more diverse is to be more inclusive: to welcome everyone with equitable tools and opportunities to succeed. A genuine welcome does not force anyone to assimilate into our norm of what we believe they should be but to welcome their individuality with compassion, as part of a collective whole with the potential to offer more because of everyone's unique contribution. Compassion, respect, empathy, or love for another does not make us weak; they make us strong.

An inclusive mindset is important to the well-being of everyone. We all need to feel welcomed. When we help others succeed, we respond to our core purpose to serve something greater than ourselves. When we have an opportunity to succeed, our well-being is also enhanced. Otherwise, we are subject to the emotional stress of exclusion, which we experience as a neural impulse as powerful and painful as a physical blow.

Love not only reduces stress it also reduces illness. Scientific studies show that patients reduced their hospital stay and subsequent need for medical care through the presence of a more compassionate physician. Love is not a weakness but a strength that enhances our capabilities, relationships, and achievements. The power of inclusion is that inclusion is not merely something we give to others but an opportunity to connect with the greater purpose of our own lives and, through that fulfillment, experience true wellness.

Compassion is easier when we accept that we are really one, more alike than unalike. A young White firefighter told me we are "one race." He was correct. According to the National Human Genome Research Institute, race is a social construct; "all human beings are 99.9% identical in their genetic makeup." Our differences are only superficial experiences that should not divide us but be opportunities for growth, creativity, innovation, and compassion. When I celebrate myself, I connect with a part of the collective whole that includes me as one of many expressions representing humanity.

In his book *Fidelity* Thích Nhât Hanh says, "[i]n true love, you don't exclude anyone.... Loving one person is an opportunity to love everyone. The deepest gift mindfulness can bring is the wisdom of nondiscrimination." Nondiscrimination liberates us to uplift the well-being of the entire world. There are many different religions, but most agree on one thing—we must love one another. The world is never appeased by hatred; it is only appeased by love. When we love our neighbors, we love ourselves.

When we have faith as lovers of the universe and as those loved by the universe and used by the universe to be loving, it does not matter what we call God. Nor does it matter who we love or who we help because we must help all beings. The question we must ask in meeting others is what I can give them to contribute to their well-being? Every real love story is a story about oneness. I am inclusive, not because you are willing to conform for me but because I am willing to accept you by respecting, accepting, and even honoring our differences.

The sacred text can be written in one word: love.

In love, there is only one religion and one political landscape: caring about one another, giving our best to make the lives of around us better. So many of our life stories carry a legacy of hurt and pain. When we share the encouragement of healing, we understand the power of including compassion, kindness, and empathy.

*Take a moment and feel compassion
and reverence for yourself.
Your mistakes and errors have contributed to who you are,
just as much as your gifts, talents, and achievements.
Fill yourself with compassion
and allow this re-connection
to embrace every being.
Breathe deeply in this embrace.
Whenever you can, take a walk,
and send this loving energy of compassion
to everyone in your midst.*

THE POWER OF INCLUSION

Giving is a Key Component of Love

Twenty years ago, I was doing a walking meditation in a labyrinth as someone began to pass out rose petals. We were all silent, focused on each step through the intricate pattern of life, passing and receiving the red petals of roses. For the first time, I realized that I did not feel as good receiving the petals as I did in giving them. In the silence, fully focused on the exchange in a meditative state, I could tell the difference. As we wound backward and forwards through the winding movement of the labyrinth, I focused more on giving more than receiving. It did not matter who I gave to either. The power that happiness gives us is not what we think it is. It is not holding on to but releasing our good. It is not greed and grabbing but savoring each moment that we can share with others.

Scientists found that amygdala activity spiked when participants perceived people in need. Not surprisingly, this was especially true for participants who scored high in empathy. This is linked to the ability to connect with and help others to personal well-being. Most humans possess a compassionate instinct, which is hard-wired in our brains. So, our amygdala can no longer be viewed as merely an alert for fear; our basest instinct is also to give. Thus, giving by opening our hearts to be more inclusive supports our well-being.

Ultimately, victory is not what we receive during our lives but what we give. Scientists have tested the most valuable memories, and experiences and they were experiences based on how people gave their time or resources to help one another, rather than what they received. For 100 days during the pandemic, I awoke at 4:00 A.M., and I led a spiritual lesson, prayer, and meditation. Sometimes I was anxious, exhausted, and had no idea what I was going to say, but for me, the experience was fulfilling and one that fortified my immune system as well as the immune systems of those who prayed for others.

A wide range of research has linked different forms of generosity to better health, even among the sick and elderly. Giving to others has been shown to increase health benefits in people with chronic illness, including HIV and multiple sclerosis. Another study found that elderly people who volunteered for two or more organizations were 44 percent less likely to die over five years than were non-volunteers. Similarly, other scientists found that those individuals who provided practical help to friends, relatives, or neighbors, or gave emotional support to their spouses, had a lower risk of dying over five years than those who did not. A study using data from thousands of adults found that people who volunteered for religious organizations reported greater happiness than people who did not volunteer for these organizations. Also, more religious volunteering made people feel, or at least report feeling, greater happiness.

THE POWER OF INCLUSION

People are happiest when their giving is coupled with a social connection, such as buying a treat for a friend and getting to spend time with the friend while they enjoy it. We are happy when we are given explicit information about how our donations are used and when we can choose how much to give. Giving is the ultimate good that allows us to serve in a manner that does not seek anything in return. If we are not generous in our willingness to accept others, we limit our ability to be our best. Giving our greatness is a shift in consciousness. When we wake up in the morning, we have the tendency to ask what we can get. Instead, we should focus on what we can give.

We can ask people what they need and look for ways to help minimize personal costs, such as giving honest feedback and making an introduction. Here's a simple exercise to get started as a connector. Start by going through your list of contacts, LinkedIn, or Facebook network. Identify pairs of people who share an uncommon commonality. Then, pick one pair a week and introduce them by email. You might also reconnect with dormant ties—not to get something, but to give. At least once a month, reach out to one person with whom you haven't spoken in years. Find out what they're working on and ask if there are ways that you can be helpful.

We can create or join a community of givers, such as ServiceSpace, the home of a series of Giftivism initiatives started by Nipun Mehta, a platform for people to increase their giver quotients, divided into three categories: gift economy projects, inspirational content, and volunteer and nonprofit support. One of the gift economy projects is Karma Kitchen, where the menu has no prices. When the bill arrives, it reads $0.00 and contains just two sentences: "Your meal was a gift from someone who came before you. To keep the chain of gifts alive, we invite you to pay it forward for those who dine after you." Kickstarter, known as the world's largest funding platform for creative projects, provides opportunities to help with designing and launching movies, books, video games, music, plays, paintings, and other products and services. On Kiva, you can identify opportunities to make microloans of $25 or more to entrepreneurs in the developing world. Both sites give you the chance to see and follow the progress of the people you help.

Pause to cultivate a giving spirit.
Where do you feel lack?
How can you recognize the best that you have
so that you can give to others?

THE POWER OF INCLUSION

Giving is Alchemy

Alchemy is the ability to take something ordinary and turn it into something extraordinary. Giving provides the gift of alchemy by moving from giver to recipient without attachment or *quid pro quo*. The magic, however, is not in the gift itself but in the energy of altruism flowing from the giver's willingness to give. The inclusive heart never stops giving, realizing that gifts will always give back—even if not from the same source, especially when given without attachment. Whatever gifts we give in welcoming others and creating safe spaces are transformations each time they are given.

How do we benefit from the power of inclusion? We receive what we give. Beyond inclusion, we expand the reach of our giving so that it is not only a gift to those who we are most comfortable with, or those few we feel are worthy of our gift—but also to those who we consider unworthy because giving is the greatest gift that we receive. Giving is not a sign of weakness but a sign of strength. Giving moves the constraints of our own awareness so that it is expanded, and in its expansion, we are open to the awareness that our good is everywhere present. When we give, the entire planet shifts with a greater embrace of who we are, what we were meant to be, and how we can improve the entire planet.

Our gifts are determined by the talents and experiences that each one of us is blessed to give. When we are inclusive, we welcome the gifts of all as part of the inexhaustible supply for the greater good of everyone, everywhere.

I really am here because of you. You really are here because of me. Our support for one another extends beyond the boundaries of tradition or decorum to provide for one another. We are always at our right time, in our right place, connected with the synergy of realizing we each bring something amazing to this journey that we call life. The lens through which we view the world is a gift. The ancestors on whose shoulders we stand are a gift. The ability to welcome and give to anyone beyond our individual experience is a gift.

We are all participants in a world that is constantly changing. The most important catalyst of change is inclusion, which is not just another word for love but also a catalyst for "miracles."

We are not here to serve our own interests. We are greater than who we appear to be in the flesh. We are greater than the place where we were born, or the tribe that we belong to, or even the dreams we have. It is only by encouraging, guiding, mentoring, uplifting, and giving to one another that we have the best experiences possible. Our support for one another extends beyond the boundaries of tradition or decorum to provide for one another. Until we learn this important lesson of the power of inclusion, we never really prosper.

THE POWER OF INCLUSION

I am grateful that my life as an African American female born in a lower economic environment in Detroit during the civil rights era gave me a compassionate lens to view the world. My ecosystem had a sense of purpose derived from the suffering of my ancestors on whose shoulders we were lifted. We were expected to be proud of our ethnicity. We were expected to be generous in supporting one another. We were expected to be strong, work hard, and put forth more than mere effort. We were expected to continue the struggle of bringing others to the table, supporting them once they got there, and giving them the opportunities we never had.

My ancestors survived the toxic energy of being welcomed and brutalized, and tortured in the process. Just a few examples of the torture by the same supremacist extremists attempting to terrorize the United States today is that enslaved Africans were whipped, hung, shot, raped, forced to have sex with immediate family members, starved after 15-hour workdays, worked to death literally, burned alive literally. Slavery in this country was not as "happy" as Hollywood depicts it. Both males and females were raped, including children. "Breaking the buck" was raping the most masculine male in front of everyone. Sometimes those who refused sex were boiled in giant containers of water, suffering before they died. So, when I witness the continued perpetration of vile violence and sexual perversion of the successors of the terrorists who enslaved Africans, I am not surprised.

The most incredible gift of inclusion is that it invites us all to heal: both harmed and harmer. None of us should carry the trauma of how our ancestors harmed others or the harm they suffered. In *My Grandmother's Hands: Racialized Trauma and the Pathways to Mending Our Hearts and Bodies,* Resmaa Menakem does some amazing work with breathing exercises, stretching, humming, and other techniques to remove the trauma from our bodies. Regardless of your background, we all carry the pain of our ancestors.

Take a moment here and now
to breathe and send love
to all of your ancestors in the past,
send strength for their suffering,
send light for their healing,
send peace for their souls,
and release them.

It is ironic that those who tortured, beat, lynched, raped, and maimed BIPOC are biased against them and believe they are more superior, civilized, and cultured than BIPOC, calling them savages. Psychologists are certain that superiority complexes only mask deep-seated feelings of inferiority, heightened under the disguise of complete self-denial.

The survival of our BIPOC community is miraculous. While there were no laws to protect us and only laws oppressing us, we were protected with the power of Spirit, supernatural forces in many situations. For example, there are accounts of enslaved African women in the 19th Century who were taught to read by Spirit. Inclusion is part of Spirit, part of the regenerative love that will heal and protect us as long as we activate it.

The Spirit that I speak of is in the church, synagogue, mosque, and temple but is not limited to holy places, worship, ancient text, or religion as it is also wherever there is despair, doubt, confusion, pain, or darkness. As Gandhi said, I am a Christian, a Muslim, a Hindu, and a Jew. Spirituality, whose Latin origin means breath or breathe, transcends religion to include everyone who has air to breathe and space to take up.

All beings, everywhere present, are united by the breath that makes us one, a breath that is the energy of love. Love is not something that we want to talk about in the workplace. It sounds corny, kumbaya, and pretentious. But love is indispensable to DEAI. Without it, the work will not get done.

*Pause to think about
how you can give your best.
How can you add
to someone's success
other than your own?
How can you volunteer
without recognition?
How can you learn that whatever
you give will be given back to you?*

Love Always Leads to Light

A book about love is the same as one about creation. God did not create the world in seven days and then stop. We are constantly co-creating, made in the image and likeness of the co-creative synergy of love. We made a choice to be here in this existence to make the world a better place. We are here to learn to see beyond our differences and help one another experience the infinite miracles of this time-space-continuum.

Deep healing is required for all of us to honor one another. We must see beyond the constructs that the past created to make some human beings believe that they are better than others. Anyone who believes they are better than another human being has deep healing to do, which starts by seeing everyone as having something amazing to share with the entire planet. We walk among the bones of ancestors who were murdered, maimed, assaulted, terrorized, bullied, and raped due to the oppression of White superiority. How can we love ourselves after those who came before us caused so much pain? How can we continue to inflict the harm that destroys our well-being?

A man sat in a prison cell with another who had done every wrongdoing against him. They both devised ways to destroy the other. Both plotted. Both hated. Both sought revenge. They counted the days, waiting for the perfect opportunity, and when it came, they attacked. Their struggle ensued as both gasped for energy. They fought and fought and tried to terminate the other until they fell, rolling and gasping for air. They struggled the entire evening until day broke, and the sun shone through the darkness of the cell. The man suddenly looked around and saw that no one else was there. The person he condemned and berated was not someone else. There was no other prisoner. The person he struck was himself.

When we take to the streets in something other than peaceful protest, with weapons to hurt others, we hurt ourselves. When we use foul language to undermine someone else, we are talking about ourselves because we are one. Anything that we do to others, we do to ourselves. When we create false narratives to justify hatred, animosity, and shame, we hurt ourselves and diminish our true potential. Any time we do not choose to operate with the pure energy of love, we diffuse our own purpose on this planet, and we marginalize the genius that we are here to tap.

Many do not believe that a path from harm to healing requires forgiveness. For me, as difficult as it may be for our trauma, without forgiveness, there is no deliverance. It cannot be stressed enough that forgiveness is not for anyone other than ourselves. If I keep focusing on someone who hurt me, I give that person my power. They, however, have moved on, oblivious to their impact. If I stay tethered to their toxic energy, I suffocate my potential in my self-imposed prison.

Love has the power to heal proactively as well as retroactively. During some of our meditation practices, we send love to our ancestors who have been harmed. We send them the strength of love and the healing energy of compassion. Through this practice, we allow ourselves to be regenerated in the power of love, as what we give, we receive.

Inclusion is a theology of grace. Scripture requires forgiveness before we go to the altar to ask for anything. Forgiveness begins with us. "Us" is the whole self, the whole city, the whole planet. We owe it to ourselves to arm ourselves with love, which is the only way to co-create the best place for future generations. Love returns peace. Love returns innovation. Love returns health. Love returns strength.

The "Beloved Community" begins within. The Beloved Community recognizes that race is a construct, and thus, we are all one family of different backgrounds, cultures, religions, lands, languages, but all one tribe with the responsibility to support one another. Loving ourselves means loving our families, our traditions, our ways, returning to the roots that gave birth to all of us. America was built by sowing seeds of hatred that have impacted our ability to love ourselves completely. Loving ourselves means honoring and reclaiming our roots by understanding them, embracing them, and reuniting with our greatness. We strengthen ourselves with the awareness of our history, to learn what has harmed us all so that it will never be repeated. But we cannot remain in the past.

Loving ourselves means doing what is necessary for self-care. The pandemic shows us the places we need to love the most, heal the most, strengthen the most. We need to cultivate a love of our BIPOC community. Oppression, animosity, and hatred breed distrust within our bodies, which creates dis-ease. How can we sew the tapestry of all our relations back together to realize that the ships that took us from one portal or the next separated our bodies but not our souls? We are one tribe of multi-cultural customs, experiences, wisdom, values, visions, and tastes—all from the same village, all from the same mother. While we are different expressions of the same seed, we must honor our entire family as one.

When love begins the process of acceptance, the synergy and synchronicity of what needs to be done will reveal itself. The first step to receiving the answer is realizing that you do not have it. The imperfection of not knowing all of the answers is something we all share, but we can connect through the opportunity to learn. When we are comfortable with not knowing everything, we re-awaken the truth that we are here to teach one another.

We must learn to trust the patience of listening, building the community of common ground, and shaping whatever it takes to fill in the gaps of what each of us needs with honor, integrity, wisdom, and respect. I love the story that Isabel Wilkerson shares in her book *Caste* of the common ground that she found with a plumber whose own bias prevented him from seeing her as worthy. She used what I call the energy of love to connect with him by recognizing something they had in common, something that would re-build the tapestry between them. After we honor our differences, we must have the courage to find common ground to unite us.

Our bodies are not merely sick from physical disease but from the spiritual oppression of not honoring our whole selves. We are all connected on the soul level. When I honor you, I honor all that I am. Honoring you begins with our history, as there can be no truth and reconciliation until we account for what has happened. Honoring ourselves begins with a deep reverence for who we all are, with radical empathy and compassion. When we open the deep wounds of harm, we will be required to be the healing balm of honesty that holds space for whatever will make us whole again.

Love gives us the tools to prepare ourselves through practices, like those here, that build our resilience. Only through the holistic honor of reverence for ourselves do we have the capacity to honor others. The good news is that by loving others, we contribute to our own well-being. The power of love does not allow us to hoard but prepares us to give until no one else is in need.

Honoring our humanity requires courage. We must open ourselves as part of the container of truth to heal what the pathology of violence, hatred, greed, and selfishness has tried to destroy. We are no longer in the wilderness of physical survival. We now have the grace of a new season to look back and acknowledge wrongs so that we can correct them. Connection takes both honesty and compassion. We are each called to be brave enough to see beyond fear to tap the powers of our differences. Fear is the only villain; love is the superhero that restores.

Honoring each other with love requires us to grow together in truth through constant education. We are ignorant of each other. Learning begins with how we hold space for what we need to know about each other with an open mind and a giving heart.

We are all invited to the table. Before we share in the meal, there is yet another step we must take together. We must share in the grace of our bounty, giving thanks for everything that has brought us to this new age of awareness. If diversity invites us to the table, equity will plate our shared meal, and accessibility will feed our bellies. But inclusion is our prayer.

Thank you, Absolute Good, for this journey that our "Grandmothers and Grandfathers," who represent all of our ancestors, took long before we were born to bring us to this table. Thank you for allowing us to be fed and protected by all our relations, even plants, animals, fish, mountains, plains, and the waters that were here long before we arrived. Mother Earth is our table, and we ask for Her forgiveness to be better caretakers of our planet and stewards for each other. In the same way that no single snowflake is alike, we are all different. But our differences bless us with the most bountiful table.

As we bow our heads, unifying the love that we share, we honor the power of being one tribe that is much bigger than our vision. We are all beings weaving an extraordinary story of the strength of our unity and the miracle of our love. Our work has just begun, but we are hopeful because we share the power that will open doors closed for so long. We thought we were here to feed the body, but we have learned to feed the soul. Our birthright is the power to stop injustice and honor the greatness within each one of us.

Every ending is a beginning.
Every closing opens the door to success.
The unknown waves us forward
in the heart of prayers,
answered before they are asked.
We are waves in this stream of absolute good,
searching for the power in which we dwell.
In every pause is something extraordinary,
an opportunity just waiting
to invite everyone in.

RESOURCES

Batmanghelidj, F., *Your Body's Many Cries for Water* (2003).
Bear, Sun & Wind, Wabun, *Walk in Balance* (1992).
Braden, Gregg, *The Science of Self-Empowerment* (2017).
Braden, Gregg, *The Wisdom Codes* (2020).
Brother Lawrence, *The Practice of the Presence of God* (1994).
Brown, C. Brené, *The Gifts of Imperfection* (2010).
Brown, Jennifer, *Inclusion: Diversity, The New Workplace & The Will to Change* (2016).
Brown, Jennifer, *How to Be an Inclusive Leader: Your Role in Creating Cultures of Belonging Where Everyone Can Thrive* (2019).
Butterworth, Eric, *The Creative Life* (2001).
Coates, Ta-Nehisi, *Between the World and Me* (2015).
Cole, Johnetta & Lott, Laura, *Diversity, Equity, Accessibility, and Inclusion in Museums* (2019).
Courageous Conversations on Racial Inclusion (2020), https://online.flippingbook.com/view/25506/.
Coyle, Daniel, *The Culture Code: The Secrets of Highly Successful Groups* (2018).
Davis, Fania E., *The Little Book of Race and Restorative Justice: Black Lives, Healing, and US Social Transformation* (2019).
DiAngelo, Robin, *White Fragility* (2018).

Dweck, Carol S., *Mindset* (2008).

Eberhardt, Jennifer L., *Biased* (2019).

Forni, P.M., *Choosing Civility: The Twenty-Five Rules of Considerate Conduct* (2019).

Frederickson, Barbara, *POSITIVITY* (2009).

"Genetics vs. Genomics Fact Sheet," National Human Genome Research Institute (2018).

Goleman, Daniel, "What Makes a Leader?, *HBR's 10 Must Reads on Emotional Intelligence* (2017).

Goleman, Daniel, *Emotional Intelligence* (2006).

Hanh, Thích Nhât, *Fidelity* (2011).

Hanh, Thích Nhât, *Living Buddha, Living Christ* (2007).

Harris, Carla A., *Expect to Win: 10 Proven Strategies for Thriving in the Workplace* (2009).

Kang, Yoona, *et al.*, "The Nondiscriminating Heart: Loving-kindness Meditation Training Decreases Implicit Intergroup Biases," *Journal of Experimental Psychology* (2013).

Kelley, Tim, *True Purpose: 12 Strategies for Discovering the Difference You Were Meant to Make* (2009).

Kendi, Ibram X., *How to Be an Antiracist* (2019).

King Jr., Martin Luther, *Where Do We Go from Here?* (1986).

King, Ruth, *Mindful of Race: Transforming Racism from the Inside Out* (2018).

Landone, Brown, *Soul Catalysts and How to Use Them* (1939).

Loving, Cecilia B., *Unbroken Circles: Holding Space, Finding Forgiveness, Transcending Edges* (2020).

Lewis, Sarah, *Positive Psychology and Change* (2016).

Lueke, Adam & Gibson, Bryan, "Mindfulness Meditation Reduces Implicit Age and Race Bias," *Social Psychological and Personality Science* (2014).

Lueke, Adam & Gibson, Bryant, "Brief Mindfulness Meditation Reduces Discrimination," *Psychology of Consciousness, Theory, Research, and Practice* (2015).

Magee, Rhonda V., *The Inner Work of Racial Justice* (2020).

Matthieu, Ricard, *Happiness: A Guide to Developing Life's Most Important Skill* (2008).

Menakem, Resmaa, *My Grandmother's Hands* (2017).

Myers, Vernā, *What If I Say the Wrong Thing: 25 Habits for Culturally Effective People* (2014).

Myers, Vernā, *Moving Diversity Forward: How to Go From Well-Being to Well-Doing* (2012).

Neff, Kristin, *Self-Compassion* (2011).

Newberg, Andrew & Waldman, Mark Robert, *Words Can Change Your Brain* (2013).

Nossel, Murray, *Powered by Storytelling* (2018).

Phillips, Katherine W., "How Diversity Makes Us Smarter," *Scientific American* (2017).

Ross, Howard J., *Everyday Bias* (2020).

Salzberg, Sharon, *Real Change: Mindfulness to Heal Ourselves and the World* (2020).

Salzberg, Sharon, *Real Happiness at Work: Meditations for Accomplishment, Achievement, and Peace* (2014).

Salzberg, Sharon, *Real Love: The Art of Mindful Connection* (2017).

Salzberg, Sharon, *Lovingkindness: The Revolutionary Art of Happiness* (2011).

Samuels, Dena, *The Mindfulness Effect: An Unexpected Path to Healing, Connection and Social Justice* (2018).

Schein, Edgar, *Humble Inquiry: The Gentle Art of Asking Instead of Telling* (2013).

Sood, Amit, *Mindfulness Redesigned for the Twenty-First Century* (2018).

Stell, Alexander & Farsides, Tom, "Brief loving-kindness meditation reduces racial bias, meditated by positive other-regarding emotions," *Motivation and Emotions* (2015).

Sue, Derald Wing, *Race Talk and the Conspiracy of Silence* (2015).

Talaga, Tanya, *All Our Relations* (2018).

Tapia, Andrés T., "Diversity 2.0: The Inclusive Leader," (2019), https://focus.kornferry.com/leadership-and-talent/diversity-2-0-the-inclusive-leader/.

Toussaint, Loren, *Forgiveness and Health* (2015).

Tutu, Desmond, *No Future Without Forgiveness* (2000).

Tutu, Desmond & Tutu, Mpho, *The Book of Forgiving* (2014).

Wall Kimmerer, Robin, *Braiding Sweetgrass: Indigenous Wisdom, Scientific Knowledge, and the Teaching of Plants* (2013).

Whitney, Diana D., *The Power of Appreciative Inquiry: A Practical Guide to Positive Change* (2010).

Yoshino, Kenji, *Covering* (2007).

Wilkerson, Isabel, *Caste* (2020).

Zajonc, Arthur, *Meditation as Contemplative Inquiry: When Knowing Becomes Love* (2008).

ABOUT THE AUTHOR

Cecilia B. Loving is an award-winning speaker, diversity, equity, accessibility, and inclusion (DEAI) thought leader, consultant, and author. Her work in restorative justice, storytelling, inclusive leadership, racial inclusion, mindfulness, and well-being helps redefine the importance of self-care and self-empowerment to create a positive and holistic environment for everyone. Her experience in uplifting the opportunity that DEAI presents for the success of organizations includes both the private and public sectors.

CECILIA B. LOVING

Cecilia has a Juris Doctor from NYU School of Law and a Master of Divinity from NY Theological Seminary, as well as a BFA from Howard University and an MFA in Theatre Management from UCLA's School of Theatre, Film, and Television. With over 20 years of experience as a lawyer in private law firms, a background in Human Rights Law, leadership as an ordained minister, experience providing DEAI leadership for both businesses and government agencies, Cecilia combines legal, analytical, and strategic skills to co-create a positive and holistic work environment. She is a winner of the National Diversity Council's 2021 Top 100 Diversity Officers Award; the New York City Department of Citywide Administrative Services' 2021 Innovation Award for FDNY's Inclusive Culture Strategy; Lawline's Top Women Faculty of 2020 Award; the City Bar Association's 2020 Diversity and Inclusion Champion Award; ABC News' First Responder Friday Award, as well as several other awards.

She has written several books *and* numerous articles and blogs, including but not limited to the following: *Good Medicine: 100 Prayers From the Pandemic; Unbroken Circles: Holding Space, Finding Forgiveness, Transcending Edges; God is a Brown Girl Too; The Gift of Going Within; Prayers for Those Standing on the Edge of Greatness; Seeing Myself as God Sees Me; God is a Lawyer Too.*

www.ingramcontent.com/pod-product-compliance
Lightning Source LLC
Chambersburg PA
CBHW030855170426
43193CB00009BA/615